No Tricks in My Pocket

PAUL NEWMAN DIRECTS

No Tricks in My Pocket

PAUL NEWMAN DIRECTS

Stewart Stern

GROVE WEIDENFELD
New York

Published by Grove Weidenfeld
a division of Grove Press, Inc.
841 Broadway
New York, N.Y. 10003-4793

Published in Canada by General Publishing Company, Ltd.

"The Glass Menagerie," by Tennessee Williams, copyright © 1945 by Tennessee Williams and Edwina D. Williams, reprinted with permission of New Directions Publishing Corporation.

"Sweet Bird of Youth," by Tennessee Williams, copyright © 1959 by Two Rivers Enterprises, Inc., reprinted with permission of New Directions Publishing Corporation.

Look Homeward Angel, by Thomas Wolfe, copyright © 1929 by Charles Scribner's Sons, copyright renewed 1957 by Fred Wolfe, reprinted with permission of Charles Scribner's Sons, an imprint of Macmillan Publishing Company.

Library of Congress Cataloging-in-Publication Data
Stern, Stewart.
    No tricks in my pocket: Paul Newman directs / by Stewart Stern.
—1st ed.
        p.   cm.
    ISBN 0-8021-1120-3
    ISBN 0-8021-3238-3 (pbk)
        1. Glass menagerie (Motion picture)   2. Newman, Paul, 1925–
    3. Motion picture producers and directors—United States—Biography.
    4. Williams, Tennessee, 1911–1983 —Film adaptations.   I. Title.
    PN1997.G533S74   1989
    791.43'72—dc19   88-31835
                                                            CIP

Designed by Irving Perkins Associates

Manufactured in the United States of America

Printed on acid-free paper

First Edition 1989

First Evergreen Edition 1991

10 9 8 7 6 5 4 3 2 1

In memory of Marjie
and all the lost sisters
and to the courage of the ones
they leave despairing

I have tricks in my pocket, I have things up my sleeve. But I am the opposite of a stage magician. He gives you illusion that has the appearance of truth. I give you truth in the pleasant disguise of illusion.

—Tennessee Williams
The Glass Menagerie

Preface

THIS BOOK WAS never intended for public scrutiny. It was never even intended to be a book. It happened like this:

Perhaps because he had been close to me for half my life and I had researched other projects for him, Paul Newman, in the spring of 1986, asked me to amass an archive that might serve as the basis for a biography, or an autobiography should he ever choose to write one. I did not know, as I went about the business of taping interviews with more than a hundred people who had known him as a toddler, or through the years of his growing and beyond, that he was contemplating a film of Tennessee Williams's *The Glass Menagerie* that he would direct and in which Joanne Woodward would appear as Amanda Wingfield.

"The play is memory," Mr. Williams states at the beginning, and since memories that summer were my business, it occurred to me, once I had discovered Paul's plan, that the exploration of Amanda's character during rehearsals might elicit from both Miss Woodward and himself certain autobiographical connections, and that just as these would cast their special light across the play and provide a special window into it, so might the play—and especially the character of the mother—provide a window into their personal histories that could become the dramatic fulcrum for the book.

The idea excited me, so I suggested that they allow me to chronicle rehearsals day by day. What I received in response were two very bleak looks across the breakfast table and the sudden, wordless clearing of the dishes.

Nevertheless, the prospect of four remarkable actors addressing themselves to a modern poetic classic under the stewardship of a director of Paul's pedigree seemed too important a conjunction of forces simply to disregard. Of course Paul disagreed entirely, protesting that because the actors had already done the play in various productions here and there, most of the exploration had been done and he would have no more to contribute than would a ringmaster with a whistle. I shrugged and said I wanted to do it anyway, and he shrugged back and said, "Be my guest," but not in a very optimistic tone.

I showed up for rehearsals as diligently as a freshman. I scratched down everything I heard or thought I heard, everything I saw or thought I saw, everything I daydreamed or imagined during the many moments of drift, about a man I had known since he was still being accosted on the streets with "Hey, Mr. Brando, my cousin in Sandusky wants your autograph," and since Miss Woodward was being introduced by Joe E. Lewis, when he spotted her from a nightclub stage, with "Ladies and gentlemen, Miss Joan Woodbury!"

There were no plans for the completed notebooks. They were to be typed and then shoved unwashed into the sealed biographical archives like two trays of summer beans into a freezer. But as the typing progressed, as I kept pressing Paul for explanations of things he had done or said that I hadn't understood, taping whatever he told me and typing whatever I taped, the material began to swell—always erratically and sometimes with considerable resistance—into its own unanticipated shape. It was very much like blowing up an innocent toy balloon and finding the whole Macy's Thanksgiving Day Parade inflating at the other end.

Paul cautioned me not to be reverential, and while I have attempted the flat, dispassionate tones of an astronaut, it would be folly to suggest that admiration had been stripped from every page. But admiration that inspires affection can inspire impertinence too, so I trust my account will prove balanced. He was most anxious not to seem "too cosmetic." I was to make him "stupider when I'm stupid and duller when I'm dull—but not just dull dull or stupid stupid—*interesting* dull and *interesting* stupid," and out of regard for him, and for the reader—whom he insists upon describing as "the audience"—I have tried. He was anxious, too, to get across "how the big issues you start out with, the big convictions, the big opposing aesthetic arguments that get between people, can all change intention and even evaporate in the course of the interpretive process. And a good idea becomes a bad idea, and a bad idea becomes something remarkable, and issues as important as the cinematic treatment of memory simply dissolve!"

While most of the dialogue comes directly from the acting edition of the play as published by the Dramatists Play Service, with certain departures based on the text as found in the New Directions New Classic, I have quoted it as spoken rather than written: a director, and others, away from their scripts and caught up in the need to communicate, will call out barn-wall approximations sometimes; and actors in the grip of passion will re-form language even as poetic as Mr. Williams's, to fit the shape of their mouths and needs. But Mr. Williams, as a man of the theatre, knew that what mattered was not the word but whether the song was truly sung, and I trust he would have understood.

I am a screenwriter, not a reporter, so there are times when I have yielded to certain temptations: to reorganize events, to complete and edit things that people said, to transpose scenes, to gather conflicts into smaller places, even to incorporate people's second thoughts as though they had been first thoughts when the principals, reviewing my second draft, offered additions I couldn't resist. But the flavor is there and it reflects a process that was very real. All participants whose words are quoted have been invited twice to correct the manuscript, but none has requested a single excision or demanded a significant change.

For their kindness in receiving me, and for allowing me a most privileged view of their process—with its lesson that the way to art is the way of the willing fool—I thank them all. And *especially* Mr. Brando—and *especially* Miss Joan Woodbury.

Stewart Stern
Seattle, 1988

Prologue

I am a guest at this rambling, whitewashed carriage house on a bend of the Aspetuck River. The Newmans bought this place thirty years ago and it's here that Joanne Woodward has been enjoying a busy hiatus since she played Amanda in *The Glass Menagerie* at Williamstown last summer. Now this Tennessee Williams classic is about to be revived at the Long Wharf in New Haven. Nikos Psacharopoulos will direct again. Karen Allen and James Naughton will repeat their roles as Laura and Jim (the "gentleman caller"). Only their Tom will be different: this time he will be Treat Williams. Rehearsals start tomorrow.

Joanne sits in her kitchen this lazy Sunday morning reading the Arts and Leisure section of the *New York Times*. She wears enormous, fuzzy pink slippers, and her Ben Franklin glasses sit aslant her nose, a safety pin through a hole in a hinge where a screw is missing. Her coffee rests before her in a cup the size of a doggie bowl, and a brown banana peel is draped across its saucer. I burst out laughing and she smiles too, wondering at this sideshow she is making of herself.

"It's always like this," she muses, for even without intending to, whenever she begins to think about a role she finds herself patching together whatever flotsam and jetsam she can find to weave a nest of physical suggestions inside of which her character can grow. Here a slipper. There a hairdo. Somebody's walk. Anything outside herself that might prod a response from within. Sometime during her draughts of cooling coffee the accent changes and I notice that in manner, attitude, and weariness of soul Joanne Woodward has yielded softly to Amanda Wingfield, and it is another person entirely who sets down the cup.

March 29, 1986 Westwood, California

Spoke with Paul and Joanne in Connecticut just now. He was hushed and short on the phone, as though the KGB were listening. He flew in last night from *The Color of Money* location after the picture wrapped in Chicago. Joanne tells me that instead of showing up unannounced for her performance in *The Glass Menagerie,* which she would have loathed, he surprised her by letting her discover him at midnight floating naked in the Jacuzzi like some elegant, pink bathtub toy when she came home by way of the garden. Spying him through the steam on the hothouse window, she thought he was a burglar and nearly took an axe to him.

She was full of helpful quotes from things she's been reading, to help me over a writer's block that's been hanging on like a cold. Did I know, for instance, that Mozart got his inspiration from driving around Vienna in an open carriage instead of sitting in an office till his head hurt?

Her idea of unemployment is what she is doing now: aside from giving eight performances of *Menagerie* a week, she's conducting acting classes for twenty-seven adoring students who appeared two years ago like limpets at high tide, stuck to her, and never went away; is directing an antinuclear play by Eve Ensler that will star Shirley Knight and is designed to be carried in a car from school to school; is filming interviews for a documentary about the Group Theatre; is guest-host for *Live at the Met;* and still finds heart-time to urge on to more exciting things a heady troika of young women—an artist, an ecologist, and an equestrian champ—all of whom happen to be her daughters. Between scenes of her play she sits in the wings knitting sweaters of hand-spun wool for practically anybody who needs one, while at the same time plotting the design of a wondrous stairway runner on which she plans to needlepoint, with the help of a battalion of friends, portraits of all the pets that have ever lived in the house, including the late Dorothy, their hen.

She couldn't talk long. Paul was shouting for her to come take a walk. Breathlessly she told me she could see three deer through the leaves from where she was standing, that the leaves were beginning to bud on the willows, and the woods across their little river were filling up with crocuses. Then she hung up.

June 4, 1986 Nook House, Westport, Connecticut

Paul and I are sitting on the screened stone porch, talking and sipping a very convincing nonalcoholic beer—bitter but no buzz. A racket of hammering comes up from the woods and jiggles the red light on my recorder: his workmen are building a bridge down there, a long, silvery, spidery span to leap the river and link this house with the big barn across the water that his artisan-handyman and friend, Jim Padula, built before he died, and where Paul and Joanne show movies and entertain. With the bridge in, they won't have to take the long way round by road.

Paul seems relaxed. His features, despite his own indifference to them, still manage to startle me.

He tells me that with the help of Boaty Boatwright at the William Morris Agency, the Newmans have been trying for some time to set up a motion-picture production of *The Glass Menagerie,* and have finally succeeded. At one point Paul had offered to put up the money himself but was advised against it on the theory that a distribution company "might have a truer experience of passion if it had money in the film it was trying to sell than if it didn't," and Paul certainly didn't want to deny any distribution company an experience of passion. But none seemed willing to exceed a "magic ceiling" of $3 million for the picture's budget, and even at his most sculpted calculation Paul knew it had to be at least $3.2 million. Then, suddenly, Cineplex Odeon came through, not only with all the money, but with "wonderful theatres to put us in where we can stay till the picture grows legs," and an executive, Garth Drabinsky, who is "only partly curmudgeon and can get off his position with generosity and grace." Joanne, Karen Allen, and Jim Naughton will repeat their theatre roles, and, Treat Williams being unavailable, John Malkovich has agreed to play Tom if the picture can be made before he leaves for China to work in *Empire of the Sun.*

One thing Paul finds terribly refreshing is that "actors still get screwed! The higher the aspiration of a film, the teenier the budget it's allowed; the teenier the budget, the less there is for the actors. So you can afford either to pay people you don't want or to ask the ones you like to do it for charity. I thought, 'Well, if all our actors aren't going to get paid anything, we should all not get paid anything equally.' So everyone's working for minimum and we're dividing my company's share of the profits six ways: actors, producer, and director will all have one-sixth of nothing. Unless of course the film's so good it doesn't have to open at the New York Public Library."

I ask him why, after the disastrous *Menagerie* with Gertrude Lawrence and the rather refined one with Katharine Hepburn, he is so anxious to direct still another version.

PAUL: Joanne asked me to. We both felt it simply wouldn't be cricket to just let it dissolve into a hiccup.

STEWART: Her performance?

PAUL: Not only hers. There had to be some record of them all. I admit I'm especially vulnerable to her, and what she does is incredibly moving. Joanne's been developing a wonderful sense of "weight" onstage, a sense of command that, in *The Sea Gull* and *Hay Fever* and now in *The Glass Menagerie*, is just dazzling to watch. Your eye simply sweeps across the stage to her and once you're there, you're caught. I have never, in the tens of times I've seen that play, believed any actress as Amanda when she says to her children, "I remember one Sunday afternoon in Blue Mountain when your mother was a girl she received seventeen gentlemen callers," except one: Joanne.

At first I didn't know what I could bring to the play, but ever since I saw it at the Long Wharf I've been jotting down ideas, challenges really, and how to solve them.

One is to see if pure Tennessee Williams works: to see if the play can really survive translation in its purest state to the screen, with no "opening up," no following Tom to the movies or Laura to typing school, which is my memory of what other versions tried to do, but simply to stay within the confines of Tennessee's characters and make cinematic virtue of claustrophobia.

I also want to see if his poetry can survive today without having to be trivialized—even though I think he was really a poet by accident. There was nothing in his personality or the way he spoke in life that named him "Poet," nothing that came across the dinner table.

Onstage it was the poetry that really created the sense of memory. We'll have to find a different way. One of the challenges I see, maybe the main one, will be to discover whether, in fact, we can create that sense of memory with film itself, and do it without being artsy. My cameraman thinks so, but I'm not sure: Michael Ballhaus, who photographed *Color of Money*. He's brilliant.

It's going to be interesting. It's all going to be interesting. To see if Malkovich can do all that narration as not-narration. To see if he can infuse it with a constantly living sense of admiration for Amanda, no matter what else he feels about her. To see how the actors can bring their stage performances down to fit the screen. All interesting.

I think it's going to be difficult for a while. They're going to feel that they're not doing anything. But it's not just a question of scale. The camera is so much closer than an audience looking at a stage that it wants more detailed performances from the actors. They won't be able to linger on the emotion, the poetry, the lyricism. They'll have to switch around quickly, be much more mercurial: when Joanne pleads with Tom to get a gentleman caller for Laura, for instance, she'll need to find a multiplicity of colors for her pleading. Her intention can't be just *to persuade*. She'll need other active verbs to support that— *amuse, allure, beguile, bully, punish*. She'll have to be pushy and beckoning, sweet and cagey, all under the banner of *to persuade*.

STEWART: Will you actually *give* the active verbs to your actors?

PAUL: No, I'll probably just say, "Make your own choices. If you want specifics, I'll give you specifics." But I prefer to let each actor discover whatever he wants to use to complicate his own performance.

STEWART: Doesn't it excite you when an actor chooses some completely unexpected way of doing something that hammers the gong of truth and sends surprise just ringing through your bones?

He narrows his eyes at me for this ossiferous allusion and gives me the withering stare he could only have learned from John Huston. "Sometimes you want surprise and sometimes you don't," he says in the flattest voice since Ned Sparks, and I leave metaphors alone.

STEWART: What is the theme of this play?

PAUL: Love. Family affection. What responsibility is. The great irony of the play is that while Tom betrays his mother and sister by abandoning them, the thing Tennessee leaves out through a kind of emotional chicanery is whether Tom's desertion has had any effect on him at all apart from the loneliness it leaves him in. Not love, not betrayal, not the guilt he feels—none of these has provided him with the energy to do anything more creative with his life than simply escape, without consequence, as if he had, in fact, gotten "out of the coffin without removing a nail."

There were more real-life consequences for Tennessee, and I think Tom is meant to be the messenger of Tennessee's experience of that period: Tennessee was simply floating from house to house with no sense of accomplishment, no self-esteem, a wanderer with nothing to publish, no way yet to put the experience into words: the terrible truth that just because you love someone it doesn't mean you can't betray them. In the play we see that Tom goes out and drinks and comes home stumbling. Tennessee doesn't say so, but I think Tom became a drunk when he went away. I think he turned into the father who deserted him as a boy, and acted out that desertion with his family, and its punishment with his life.

STEWART: If he's a drunk, could the gentleman caller be a drunk also?

PAUL: It's only a cast of four, Stewart!

STEWART: Well, have you thought about the relationship between Tom and the gentleman caller and why Tom chose him as the only man he ever brought home to his sister? Was it one alcoholic doing a favor for another? Was it a favor between two homosexual lovers? After all, Tom's gay and the gentleman caller's not married. Is his "girlfriend" just a ruse? All Tennessee gives you is that he's a "nice, ordinary young man."

PAUL: I don't think this can suffer that kind of examination. I certainly wouldn't try. The only thing Tom's homosexuality does is that sometimes it shuts him down. Complete openness in everything but that. It's the thing that makes him claim he goes "to the movies," the idea that he's doing things out there that he's ashamed to tell Amanda or his sister.

STEWART: I've never seen Tom played as homosexual.

PAUL: Well, Malkovich wants to explore it.

STEWART: Do you see Amanda as Tom's destroyer?

PAUL: I see her as a person whose appetite is too big, who asks more than anyone can fulfill, or *should* fulfill. No one should be asked to keep other people alive. Tom shouldn't be asked to keep his sister Laura alive. He can't provide what his mother thinks are Laura's needs. Amanda has to be the provider—a dual provider: she has to provide both the sustenance and the illusion that keep them all going.

One thing Karen Allen will bring to Laura, which I don't want to tell her she brought to the play or she'll get too self-conscious, is a wonderful sense of resignation without bitterness, of the acceptance of loneliness and defeat. And she does it with such grace. She accepts with such grace that she's "peculiar," and that her life will have to be lived in fantasy, through old phonograph records and little glass animals, forever.

STEWART: On the stage, Karen's Laura was like a woman on her deathbed trying to be an absolutely wonderful hostess.

PAUL: When the gentleman caller goes it's going to be very interesting to find out how many different ways she can play the impact of his leaving, because I can think of about six. If what's left is the memory of his kiss, which she will carry to her grave, there is nothing lost or wasted. If what's left is terror of the future, it becomes something else. Amanda feels that terror. So whatever choice Karen makes will dictate who will be comforting whom at the end.

But it's memory. Memory. How do you invoke memory on the screen? How do you invite the audience to participate in the exorcism of that memory? Those are the most important questions for me. Remembering, and exorcising what he remembers, are the reasons why Tom's there, why he takes us there, why there's even a play. When he leads us up to his old boarded-up apartment at the beginning, he'll be drinking because of that memory and because of what he will have to endure by confronting it before he can leave it behind. I want to dramatize the waste in him, the waste since that memory has haunted his life. When he leaves at the end and says, "Blow out your candles, Laura, for nowadays the world is lit by lightning—and so goodbye," he won't be saying goodbye to the audience as he usually does in the theatre. He'll be saying goodbye to the memory, to the plague of guilt that has haunted him, the reproach from within for having abandoned his sister, which grief had only partially relieved.

STEWART: Will you have him frankly acknowledge the camera?

PAUL: Oh, yes. In fact, at the beginning I'm going to let the camera be the audience. It will follow him like a dog. He'll walk away, then turn to wait for it to follow, and not start walking again till it's nearly caught up. He'll try to get into the abandoned tenement where the family once lived—we found a wonderful one in East Harlem, incidentally—but the front door's been boarded up, so he goes around to the side, climbs up the fire escape to this completely derelict apartment.

We'll shoot all that on location, at dusk, which seems to me to be the color of memory. Then we'll match that light on the soundstage as he actually comes in. And as he's walking through you'll hear shattered window glass breaking on the floor, see the dusty shreds of things they once owned hanging wherever they left them. He comes out through the kitchen window onto the fire escape again, the real one at the actual location, just to begin his monologue. Then as he goes back in, we'll wipe on some object close enough to the lens to black out the screen, and continue to wipe on the soundstage set of the apartment, but now the way it looked when they still lived there.

STEWART: You melt through?

PAUL: Yes, start going through walls. So when he reaches that part of the monologue when he's describing his father "who fell in love with long distance," the camera will simply slide off him into what we assume is the derelict apartment of today but which has become, just for an instant at first, the apartment of his memory. Shafts of reflected light become the glass menagerie. Laura's face comes into view as she gathers up one of her little glass animals and brings it up to the light. The camera goes past her and there is Amanda, on the telephone, talking. Then it moves in a complete circle to examine the little sun-room where Amanda's plants are hanging in the feeble light, the phonograph, the typewriter, the faded, beaded things that separate the dining room from the parlor, then up over the picture of the father, and as you pan across that wall to black, in another wipe that brings you into the present, we're on Tom's face again as he says, "The last we heard of him was a picture postcard from the Pacific coast of Mexico, containing a message of two words: 'Hello—Goodbye!' and no address," and as he's saying that, the voice of Amanda seeps in for the first time. You can't distinguish the words yet, but as he invokes the memory, as he actively seeks it, the words come clear and you cut right to Amanda's face. Then you're in the past to stay till Tom comes out. I think that's fairly nifty.

STEWART: When *does* he come out? Just at the end?

PAUL: No, on his next monologue. All the monologues will be in the present looking back on himself in the past.

STEWART: And are you going to use sound to invoke memory, too? Will you hear the life of the tenement and the alley in those memory sequences, or will you cut out all allusion to anything but those four characters?

PAUL: Well, you might hear giggling in the alley and people tripping over trash cans, but I don't think you'll ever see another person, except maybe the shadows of people next door at the Paradise Dance Hall. It's going to be pretty straightforward, particularly in terms of camera movement, except for a couple of circles I want to make around Joanne in her "Jonquils" speech, to really isolate her in the rapture of that memory.

Now, this has nothing to do with what we've been talking about, but I want to see Tom witness the Gentleman Caller scene, I want to see him watching when Laura and the gentleman caller think they're alone. In the play he never watches, but I don't see any reason for that scene unless he witnesses it. How can it be his memory if he wasn't there?

As far as the ending is concerned, the best thing I've got is Malkovich and his emotion, which is extremely accessible to him and is absolutely critical to that scene. So often onstage you see the actor begin pumping himself up to reach the emotion at the end. That can't be. It will simply have to attack him. He should have absolutely no resistance against it. Actors kill for a scene like that. I've played it in my head a dozen times and I know it's uncontrollable for me. That's why I may ask John to sit on it. You've got to sit on that emotion and not let it happen until it just explodes out of you, and I want it to happen only once, because as you know, I'm a great one for emotional economy. If your instrument is tuned well enough it will catch you by surprise. Just a sudden image, I don't care what it is, I don't care what John finds to trigger the effect, it can be anything. The words of the script alone are enough for me. I mean, I can turn it on in the bathroom like a faucet! So he'll have to sit on it till the moment it happens, but with John I know it will.

Then, as he begins to regain some control and says, "Blow out your candles, Laura," I'll go off him to black, and the second we hit black you'll see Laura's face come into that black shot, she'll pick up the candle, blow out the flame, put it down, and then maybe I'll pull back to show Amanda with her. But as I say, I'm not certain yet who will be comforting whom. I'll stay on them just for a second, then cut back to the derelict apartment of today, just shooting up at a wall with Tom's figure against it. You won't even see his face. He says, "And so goodbye," and the picture ends.

STEWART: Beautiful.

PAUL: Let's shoot it.

STEWART: The big dramatic question for me about the whole movie is, how and why has Tom reached the point where he needs to seek this memory, and have it exorcised before witnesses on this particular day, at this particular dusk? If he can reach back into the past and get Laura to blow out those candles, how will that free him, what will it free him from? How will he be able to walk away from this derelict place in a way different from the way he led us there?

PAUL: Do you want to write that, Stewart? Tennessee didn't. It's a confessional, simply a confessional. I don't know how it can be anything else. Tom confesses to the audience and leaves them with this incredible emotional jolt at the end that I can't even read on the page without choking up.

STEWART: Maybe that's reason enough to do it and why it's good that it's you.

PAUL: Well, whatever.

September 20, 1986 Nook House, Westport, Connecticut

Paul is now addicted to licorice jelly beans. He carries them in his car and rations them out to me three a day, dropping them into my waiting palm from a hole in his fist, as if he were some great International Famine Fund and I were Ethiopia.

Something has happened and I am sitting here on a rock in the woods above the sparkling little river, grinding my teeth. Rehearsals for *The Glass Menagerie* are to start in three weeks and until just now Paul had agreed that I could watch the whole process in order to write down my observations of how he works. But when I told him a few minutes ago that I'm off to Seattle to see my wife and will be back in time to ride to the studio with him on his first day of rehearsal, he suddenly amended our agreement. Now he doesn't want any observers there till he and his actors "are used to each other"! Doesn't he understand the importance of that first day to any chronicle of a director's journey? "Well, it never bothered a cast to have me around before!" I protested to him, but he pointed out that those had been my scripts that we were filming and as the writer I had to be there. Why does this reasoning fail to persuade me? I find myself angry at him for changing his mind, and at myself for deferring so easily. Is it his stardom that has silenced me?

October 5, 1986 TWA Flight 708

Paul called me in Seattle to say, "Forget about all that 'first-day' stuff I said. Come to New York, it's fine." So I did. The landing wheels are down.

First Day of Rehearsal

We are on Stage I in the bowels of the Kauffman Astoria Studios, once the old Famous Players—Lasky lot that my uncle, Adolph Zukor, built in 1916. I remember being told as a boy how he brought the king of Siam here one day on his speedboat, the *Lottie K.,* to watch the filming of some silent epic, and how the admiral of the Siamese fleet, who didn't know the lock on the bathroom door was broken, made the cruise down the East River memorable for my mother by walking in on her in the john and then bowing out backward, because in Siam it was rude to turn your back on a lady no matter what she happened to be doing.

I make my way through a maze of basement workshops and find everyone gathered in the cavernous rehearsal hall studying a model of the set. Paul is leaning on the six-foot shepherd's crook he will keep with him throughout the rehearsals: he has crashed his race car on a rainy track and broken two ribs, but he is embarrassed about it so I don't ask how he feels. He is getting a terrible cold and looks drawn and nervous, the way he does before any challenge, but he embraces me and tells me to sit at the table where the cast will read.

Because he must go to Atlanta several times between now and the shooting, to test his car and race, he will have only twelve days of rehearsal in which to forge a family from the people in this room and to make all the aesthetic and technical decisions demanded by the transfer of a classic text to the screen.

All business, he says, "Let's begin," and everyone sits down. Perfunctory introductions, no welcoming speeches. Joanne, chatty and toting the big bag in which she lugs around her life, sits beside him. John Malkovich is to her right, then Karen Allen. Jim Naughton, across from them, places empty chairs on either side of him to establish the apartness of his character. At the corner next to Paul, Michael Ballhaus, the cameraman, is all in black, a costume he will not alter for our entire time together in order to stay, like a puppeteer, "a part of the background." Occupying a corner opposite Paul is the person he will come to rely on most to keep his thoughts in order: Mary Bailey, the script supervisor. I sit behind her, away from the table. Burtt Harris, the producer, a solid, sensitive man of long experience in film production management, and his talented young associate producer, Joe Caracciolo, whose father was head propman for Paul on *Rachel, Rachel,* withdraw. Paul sneezes volcanically and mutters, "Good Lord! I could have killed a squirrel at fifty feet with that!" And everyone laughs, unknotting.

PAUL: When I decided to direct this I said to Joanne, "There ain't nothing to do but get everyone together then watch from the wings with a baton." But the more I got into it, the more brilliantly the ideas flowed, until the margins of my script were black with them! The most insightful notes! The most marvelous sketches! Notions that were absolutely staggering! Then someone broke into my car and stole the whole damn thing.

And so the only script he has now is the little blue acting version of the play put out by the Dramatists Play Service and Xeroxed on big paper to accommodate his notes. There is no screenplay at all and no one will get credit for one.

PAUL: Before we start, I'd like to settle a really weighty question. Should we have a consensus about accents?

JIM: When we did it at the Long Wharf I had a kind of southern version of a Midwest twang.

PAUL: Keep it. Hard *r*'s. To separate you as an outsider. The gentleman caller's the only one not from the South.

He turns to John Malkovich.

Two things, John. A sense of exorcism and confession. And drink, to whatever extent you want to use that. And as we go through, try to discover what will make you accept the camera as your confidant.

Malkovich questions some minor inconsistency of grammar within a speech, diverting Paul's broader attention to a tiny point of focus where he doesn't want it to be. "Change it," Paul says shortly, and nods for him to go on.

John begins to read.* His voice is velvety, insinuating, sensual as caramel melting on a sill in the sun. It seems to issue from somewhere behind his nose. Paul stops him almost immediately to add a further thought:

* See Appendix for a synopsis of the play.

PAUL: John! Don't let yourself find the memory too soon. Actively pursue it. Seek ghosts. Voices. Invite them to populate this place again! Do anything you can to move Tom into the past and take us with him. Once you're on your feet you can try everything—you can look at the camera directly and it will follow you, it'll go wherever you lead it. At least we'll try. I want to be very careful not to violate the play just to give a performance with the camera, but if it works it works, and if it doesn't it might lead us to a better idea. Ain't nothin' written in concrete. Go ahead.

Malkovich starts again. He is balding, but above his collar there is a vestige of what looks like a tiny blond punker pigtail that seems the statement of some mystery I have no inclination to solve. He has a mustache and beard, and there's string tied around one wrist. White stockings and black espadrilles give him the curious padded gait of a coolie. When Joanne's Amanda tells his Tom to chew his food leisurely, "Chew, chew!" his explosive reaction startles me.

As they read I write notes: "P.N. in tan cords, navy and white striped shirt. Cold metal chairs. Blueprint of set on table. Joanne graceful in long checked skirt. Tinted rimless glasses. Hair permed. She's absolutely forthright, as if to say: 'This is my face. This is my hair. See? It's *gray!*' Beautiful, mischievous, heartbreaking eyes shifting colors, swift as the sea. Has everyone looking for safety pins now so she can keep track of her knitting.

"Karen Allen. Tiniest hands and wrists! Luminous talent. Small package. Little freckled face, warm as a chestnut.

"Naughton: lovable. Fun-loving as a Rover Boy. Seasoned pro. Tender eyes.

"Paul sits on a special chair, the kind seen used with computers, padded for kneeling, on rollers—gift from Joanne to ease pain of accident and make a game of it. He frowns as he listens to John, arms folded across chest, hair clipped short as though for a voyage, unadorned as a spy."

My mind drifts. I wonder at the generosity of the caterer's buffet in the corner of this boiler room of a stage. It has a white cloth and bears platters of fresh fruits and fancy cheeses, nuts, home-baked breads and muffins, crudités and dips, ice tubs filled with juices, pyramids of cakes, urns of coffee and tea, a feast of snacks to support the sense of fellowship and to lighten anxiety. Most productions offer only Danish and doughnuts, but this display reflects the Newmans' style: generosity beyond the requirements, manifesting concern for others through a trail of treats and small surprises. The toy model of the set looks as snug as a hobbit's house and I want to crawl in. Its floor plan has been laid out in tape all over the battleship gray floor of this dungeon so the actors can know what rooms they're supposed to be in. Against one wall stand the following: an ancient stove connected to nothing, a deep sink with a slimy drain for wringing out mops, and a stained white refrigerator of a sort that might contain the bodies of dead dogs in some high school biology lab. The lights thirty feet above my head are fluorescent, and as cold as embalmers' lamps.

Paul makes notes as they read, in his pinched half-printed writing. There are nails on his fingers now. I remember when they were chewed to the quick and as purple as naked birds. John smokes during his second monologue. He pronounces "the" as "thee," "a" as the A in ABC, and after every "the" or "a" he pauses, calculating the word that follows as if it were a crevasse he had to leap. It gives him an odd, loping, halting delivery. I remember Paul asking him to "wrench the rhythms" of the poetry: perhaps this is the product of that request.

Whenever anyone upstairs flushes the toilet, water bangs and hisses through the pipes, and I have the illusion that I'm riding a damaged submarine falling quickly down through the sea.

Malkovich purrs on softly, politely, but he laces his reading with those sudden, unpredictable eruptions that startle me time after time. His beard, his pallor, the rich languor he creates, give a persona to Tom that is ripe with innuendo and evocative of the young Tennessee: watchful, heavy-lidded, bemused, but with a capacity for terrifying conflagration that the Tennessee I met once could only write about. I think this performance will challenge Joanne. Many of the Toms I have seen, including the one played by Eddie Dowling (in the first New York production with Laurette Taylor), have tended to be "effects"; they provide only a mood and leave the performing to Amanda. But this Tom promises complexities: he is at once satirical, manipulative, furious, subversive, and enslaved. How will Joanne respond? I wonder as I watch her knit. She hardly looks at him, but her eyes, never straying from the needles, let me know she is wise to his artistry, appreciative but alert, and ready for action. Even in this reading she's in character. "When I go onstage," she has told me, "and I have that terrible feeling of 'Oh, it's not there tonight!' I put an invisible doorway out in front of me and I just step through, and on the other side I'm who I'm supposed to be."

John isn't trying for the humor yet, and hasn't revealed much humor in himself, but this is the first day, and I sense that he and Paul, because they are both directors, will be circling and sniffing each other out, stiff-legged, until they are surer.

Paul sits high on his kneeling chair, frowning deeply, listening to his actors and trying to figure out what to do or say. Their reading seems hurried and perfunctory, but it is the long, necessary clearing of a throat before the song, and Paul lets it run its course. If it were material new to everyone, this might be a time of fervent exploration for these actors, but they have come to an old fire and are just beginning to warm their hands again.

They have read through the Quarrel scene, where Tom bursts from the apartment after calling his mother "an ugly, babbling old witch!" and now it is morning and he has apologized. And when she asks him where he goes at night and he answers, "I go to the movies," John lets me understand that the adventures Tom seeks have less to do with the allure of the screen than the enticements of the balcony. It is a fresh revelation for everyone, and the actors become more engaged and alive. They are starting to explore each other now in a way that is very real. Joanne's Amanda promises to be, for all her southern frailty, strong and tough and practical, striking hard bargains with a son who is her match. The cruel bones of the play come clean in their voices, but its tenderness is fragmentary still; there are glimpses of it from time to time, whenever they can tear their eyes from the page and look at each other.

It is midmorning when they reach the Annunciation scene. Paul's frown is so intense that it has driven all the blood from his brow. But now as Joanne, thrilled by the preparations she must make for the gentleman caller's arrival, begins bustling about the whole apartment without ever moving once from her chair, Paul lets himself smile. In the delicacy and pity with which Tom breaks to Amanda the truth she has known forever but has never wanted to face, that her daughter Laura is crippled and "peculiar," John invests Joanne with the fragility of glass, and I am aware, simply from his reading of the line, that the family itself is the glass menagerie, with Laura the most breakable of all. But is she really, or is Tom? John's portrayal subsides at times into the exhausted ironies and weary croakings of a ravaged old queen, then, as in the Drunk scene, he revives to entertain with all the silly optimism of a clown with no reason to hope.

I wonder when Karen will begin to let us see the Laura for whom Tom suffers so much. Her stage performance was remarkable for its absence of that wistfulness into whose trap so many well-intentioned Lauras have tumbled. This one asks for no pity. Karen is running in neutral, reading in a hoarse monotone, assessing where she is, and studying Paul. All this while Michael Ballhaus has been listening entranced, his expression dreamy, his smile constant, nodding encouragement to anyone whose eyes meet his gaze.

At the entrance of the gentleman caller, Paul jots down a note. Once the actors are on their feet he will whisper his remarks to Mary Bailey, and she will record them as reminders for him when he talks to the cast between scenes. When they are up from the table, he will be on his feet too, prowling the sidelines, giving body English to every move they make. At times Joanne is leathery in her power, like her Aunt Dae-Dae from Atlanta; at others, warbling like a happy bird, she's all tinkling lemonade, white wicker, summer porches, all echoes of her beloved child—her own mother.

In the midst of the Gentleman Caller scene, that long *pas de deux* that Karen and Jim once infused in the theatre with the intricacy of French lace, John Malkovich begins suddenly to compare two different versions of the play. What can he have found that he is studying with such intensity? He lifts his head once, swiftly, as though some scent had come to him, then puts on his glasses to inspect his fellow actors. Now digging distractedly at the edge of a quarter with his workingman's thumb, he hops onto the back of his chair and surveys the proceedings with the pinpoint focus of a monkey on a flea, appraisingly and with a director's eye. Paul notes it and frowns. Jim Naughton grows funnier as he warms to the scene, making Joanne look up from her knitting and laugh at his energy and bluster. Paul rises. Everyone looks, expecting him to speak, but he has only gotten up to massage the pain out of his side. The reading goes on.

John sees that he has reached his final monologue and puts his script away to try to recite it by heart. Absorbing his emotion in an activity by tracing designs on the tabletop with the lid of his yellow felt pen, he stares through the script's closed cover and speaks his final lines as though they had just occurred to him. He dodges the trap of the poetry, and what he does with "Blow out your candles, Laura," while only a peddler's sample of what he intends to bring, moves us all. Paul hasn't had to tell him to "sit on it." The reading of the play is finished.

They all start talking at once. Karen, Joanne, and Jim, all closely linked as veterans of Williamstown and the Long Wharf and by the friendship born there, agree that it is very strange to have to start from scratch, for the screen, with material that had become second nature on the stage—having, in a way, to pretend they have never done it. As their chatter and laughter fill the room, John Malkovich, who is the outsider here, masks whatever exclusion he may feel with a professorial, almost fussy preoccupation that finally carries him to Paul with the versions of the scripts he has been comparing clutched in either hand. He's concerned about the Quarrel scene, he says in his soft, sibilant way. In the earlier version, published just after the play first opened on Broadway, the scene is described as beginning in the midst of a fight already in progress, whereas in the later version, Williams motivated the fight by adding an opening beat* in which Amanda picks at Tom to correct his posture.

JOHN: I think it's better in this script he wrote right after the
       first production. What he stuck in later that leads to the

---

* A "beat" is a unit of a character's action within a scene, just as an "action" is a unit of a character's overall goal or "intention" within the play. The "intentions" motivate the play, and it is in their collision that conflict occurs.

quarrel doesn't really fit with the quarrel. It's better to start in the middle, the way they did it originally.

PAUL: Isn't that sudden?

JOANNE: I think it's a very good idea! That beginning was always a problem to act. I don't know why we have to justify our fight before it happens.

She walks away to the buffet as though the matter were settled. The others have gathered there too, buttering hunks of Irish soda bread and debating about where to have lunch. John lingers patiently beside Paul, watching him pore over the two versions of the script.

JOHN: It's better. Shorter, subtler, more poetic. Of course I don't know if that's what you want to do—

He has started adding little modifying tags to his suggestions, as if to assure Paul that he defers to his director's authority and that his suggestions imply no challenge, but I wonder if it isn't a mask. John waits for Paul's answer, but deep in his own preoccupations Paul seems to have forgotten all about him. Paul straightens up suddenly, leaving the scripts where they lie and abandoning John, and announces in a voice too loud for the room that there's a lot of work to do but he doesn't want to do it too quickly. Is this his answer to John? It's hard to know just whom it's meant for. He speaks without looking at anyone. It's as if he were addressing passengers on an enormous ocean liner in the ways of lifeboat drill. He will meet the actors during lunch, he says in that declamatory voice, one by one, on this stage! Then he turns to Drew Rosenberg, the production assistant, and requests the "half a tuna sandwich on rye" that will become his daily meal. He seems unnerved. Quietly John reclaims his scripts and walks away. Perhaps Paul told him he'd think about it.

Unlike many directors trained in the Method, Paul thinks that sitting around a table, reading and discussing character day after day, simply postpones the work, and the frightening exposure that can only be lived through by *doing* the work. He likes to cram the reading into the first morning and put the script on its feet that afternoon. To familiarize the actors with the actual set, still under construction on Stage H, he leads them there while lunch is on its way so that when they return these tape lines on our floor will hold the memory of real rooms for them.

I troop with them through the labyrinth of workshops, down corridors, and up smelly flights of stairs to where Tony Walton's set is being built. It stands like a Thai stilt house, high above the floor on a platform of raw pine, to allow for entrances up the stairs and fire escape from below, as Paul desires. We stumble through the unfinished rooms, getting familiar with the shape and size of things. John fondles the wainscoting of his bedroom wall, which hasn't been aged yet, trying to visualize how it will look. Joanne admires the "character" pressed-tin moldings with which Tony has crowned the apartment. They still wear their workshop shine but a few have been "atmosphered" to the color of drying blood, suggesting that the whole place will appear to be as wounded as the characters it houses. Joanne turns from it, eyes grayed and sad, and I feel a heaviness like grief as I drag through the rooms. Jim and Karen stand bookending the fireplace, unaware of their perfect symmetry. When each touches an end of the mantel at the same moment, it is as if they had touched fingertips, and their eyes engage and they smile. This parlor will belong to them as to no one else in the play, and the glow of the candles Jim brings to it will light the play's heart. I look around for Paul but I can't find him.

Suddenly we are hurrying after him through the halls, like a gang of medical students on grand rounds. I can see him at the head of the column, marching along very fast. He turns to Jim Naughton and says something I can't hear. I see Jim look bewildered. "Tracing!" Paul says with enough intensity for me to hear him. "Tracing! Tracing!" Jim doesn't know what he means but he thinks he should, so he smiles and nods like someone with water in his ear, pretending he's gotten the message. It's an expression I've seen on my own face in the mirrors I pass while walking with Paul on the street when he gives me aloud two words of some thought he has said in his mind and thinks he's delivered in full. Frequently his communications are not only carved down to a minimum—as so much else in his life is too—but are actually missing in places, like failures in the transatlantic cable when it was all we had for our overseas calls. The eccentricity is endearing, but I can see how it could drive an actor nuts. Can Paul mean that Jim's gentleman caller should have the habit of tracing shapes in air?

I ride in the Teamster's station wagon with Joanne. She has invited me to use our first lunch break for a commando raid on a health-food store so she can stock up on light edibles with which to pacify herself during rehearsal without caving in every ten minutes to the temptations of that magically self-replenishing buffet. She wanders from rack to rack collecting packets of things in cellophane brittle with age, peering longingly through one dusty wrapper after another in the hope that whatever crumbling, ricey thing there is inside will somehow taste like a peanut butter sandwich. The basket gets heavier and heavier. She pays when she can't carry any more, with a highwayman's wad of bills, and makes the proprietor's day with her friendliness. No encounter is wasted. Life never stops. I have no idea what she and Malkovich thought of each other. She never even mentions *The Glass Menagerie*.

We come back to the rehearsal hall and find Paul still caught in the worried hush of a conference, his sandwich untouched. Actors have been coming to him one by one like confessors to a priest, and he has conferred with them briefly. He speaks with Mary Bailey now as to an aide-de-camp, in an urgent broken whisper. There's something doomed about him, like a field commander whose battle has swung the wrong way, and I cannot imagine what's wrong. He has an eerie ability to blot up his own sound when he wants to so no one outside the radius he sets can hear him. It seems to have something to do with linking arms. He needs to take your arm when he confides. His voice travels marrow to marrow.

Midafternoon. Paul has begun to "put the play on its feet." He began the afternoon by working intensively with Malkovich on the first monologue, frequently interrupting himself to hear from Michael Ballhaus about the shots he has planned in his mind, which soon captivate them both, but confiding again and again his worry about getting "artsy-fartsy." Now he has moved to the first Dinner scene. He drags a couple of metal chairs to the portion of the floor labeled "Dining Room" and seats Joanne and Karen where the table is supposed to be. John joins them, bringing his chair. They pantomime the activities of dining, and we are told a table is on its way. Michael is at Paul's shoulder, murmuring ideas to him and framing camera angles with his hands. When Paul begins blocking out the action of the scene, Malkovich's eyes never leave him. The women could open on Broadway tonight, they seem so comfortable: their lines are still in their heads from last summer, so they work without scripts. Malkovich holds on to his, although he refers to it very little. Carrying it may serve as a signal to Paul not to tie him down before he's ready. Paul seems very anxious to set things, but John is a walking warning. Politely, he will insist throughout rehearsals on testing all the paths, and will never reveal completely which he has chosen until he performs it for the camera. Paul takes note of John's script with the smallest hint of laughter in his eyes.

He stops the scene midway to stare at the floor. In the silence that follows, Mary Bailey brings him the notes he has whispered and waits for him to take them, but he seems unaware of her. Minutes go by. He shakes his head and groans. He massages the scars on his fingers, souvenirs of a motorcycle spill in the rain long ago. Then he looks up.

PAUL: Where are we? Should we talk about details? Yes we
    should. So. Joanne, make a Kazan transition on the "Chew,
    chew, chew!" so Amanda never stops talking.

Elia Kazan, in directing *Sweet Bird of Youth,* taught Paul how to arrive at the emotion coming up in the second "beat" of a scene by beginning the transition into it while still in the middle of the first, so he never had to stop to make the shift and the momentum of the play was uninterrupted: a skier shifting his body into a turn before his skis have even reached it.

PAUL: Also, Joanne, you might have fun if you demonstrate "Eat
    leisurely."

And he acts it out, smiling ecstatically, a ghost of Epicurus rolling ambrosia around in his mouth. Everyone laughs, relieved.

JOANNE: Should I do wonderful things in the kitchen first, or
    just start talking at the table?

PAUL: Do wonderful things in the kitchen. Again! Whole scene.

They begin. Paul stops them right away.

PAUL: John! Startle her! Skid your chair back. Make a racket.
Stop the scene if you want her attention. And don't direct
your whole speech to her—don't indulge her that way. You
did a wonderful thing before when you were brushing off
your clothes. Extend that. Use the brushing whenever you
want to brush *her* off. Go on!

If brushing works, John will invent a different way. He pecks
with his head over the table like a vulture savaging a corpse as he
yells, "It's you that makes me hurry through my meals with your
hawklike attention to every bite I take!" It's a bizarre choice and
it's wonderful. Joanne is playing full-out now. Paul seems hyp-
notized by her. As he half reclines on the battered couch, boots
crossed, shepherd's crook hooked over his shoulder and pressed
to his cheek, his adoration is like an unguent in the room, so
naked, so private that my impulse whenever I see it is to turn
away.

But I see his eyes glaze as he watches her, his mind drifts, and
all at once he is on his feet and talking to Michael again. His
concentration seems so perforated that I don't know what he's
doing. I'm accustomed to seeing him struggle to find intentions
for his actors, or to convey some vision to his cameraman, or to
worry the thousand conflicting needs of an eager staff into a
cohesive plan, but I have never seen him as scattered or uncertain as he seems this afternoon. The actors are holding their own
but seem increasingly bewildered as they are asked to start and
stop a dozen times while he flits from branch to branch, unable
to rest long on any one: now it's the camera, now the scale of
performance; now he's urging them to stay loose till they "find

the impulse"; now the setting of positions has priority. He is neither staging nor allowing them to discover for themselves the roads from their own motivations to movements that flow naturally from them. What's happening here?

Now suddenly he's standing over there, by the model of the set, staring into all its little cardboard rooms as if they might yield answers. Yet he doesn't even seem to be seeing it. Is it a mandala for him to center on? Is it like John Huston's cigar? Paul used to tell me, "I thought Huston's whole inspiration came out of that cigar, that somehow he knew that if he could get away from everybody and just roll that cigar around long enough, he could suck his whole plan out of it, it was all locked up in there. Then he'd get done rolling and just stroll on back to the set and start giving orders about things he'd had no notion of five minutes before."

Michael Ballhaus has joined him at the model, looking for some signal that all is well with him. I can't hear what they're saying, but Michael seems to be expressing again, in a most emphatic way, his own aesthetic opinions, and I think he may be trying even now to excite Paul with his ideas for creating a dream on film within this cramped apartment, for painting with light and orchestrating with movements of his camera his vision of how memory might look. But the discussion seems mistimed under the circumstances, and I know that Paul, even when entirely the master of his focus, is too conservative to support such a vision entirely; it might seem excessive to him and he would seek ways to modulate and shape what Michael is offering in a way his own taste could accommodate. But today he cannot respond, though he tries to listen. While the affection the men found for each other on *The Color of Money* persists, it will become increasingly clear that the ideas they hold, while cousinly, don't kiss: Michael's vision swirls with images and motion while Paul's is essential and still:

Jack Sprat could eat no fat,
His wife could eat no lean;
And so, betwixt them both
They licked the platter clean.

Joanne's cheery soprano breaks Paul's communion with the model. She, who can flash in and out of character more swiftly than a butterfly darting through a gate, is now whipping around on Paul's kneeling chair like crippled Porgy on his cart, singing as she shoots around the room: "Bess, you is my woman now!" The voice is terrific, but the lyrics, coming from a mouth that is stuffed with those virtuous rice cakes, sound as if they're being crooned into the flank of a bear.

Paul calls for the second part of the scene. He seizes Malkovich and propels him to the imaginary rack where Tom's coat will hang; he wants him to find his cigarettes in its pocket. The actor goes limp on his arm, as if to say to everyone, "See, I'm just a puppet in his hands!" But he has made it clear already that as a student of this play, and as a director, he may consider himself more experienced about its possibilities than Paul.

Paul wants the dinner to end with a move to the parlor, where they can have coffee and find "enjoyment and relish of the hearth," as he puts it, following Tom's eruption from the table. Paul believes that offering coffee in the parlor can have a ritual, as well as a healing, effect: "There's something very southern about it," he thinks, and he wants the family settled around Amanda when she recites for the hundredth time her memory of that Sunday afternoon in Blue Mountain when the seventeen gentlemen callers came to pay court. But John wants to smoke on the fire escape so he doesn't have to endure her peroration. He has learned that the windows on the set will actually open, and is thrilled with the notion of darting along the fire escape outside while being able to toss his comments through window after window as he goes.

PAUL: If you play it through the windows it looks aimless.

JOHN: I think it's too short a scene to do "southern style" in the parlor.

PAUL: But it's going to be a terrible stretch for the camera to even keep you in the shot! Why don't you use the fireplace if you're going to smoke, or maybe Tom doesn't smoke at all and just keeps exhaling hopelessness. "Can't smoke in here, can't drink in here, can't eat in here!"

JOHN: I think he always smokes outside, and he doesn't want to listen to his mother. He wants to hear about the vulgar, the sexy, the dirty—who was doing it to whom—not this light entertainment about gentlemen callers. He'd sit with his face on the table and his hands over his ears, or get outside. I can't imagine him even staying in a room with Amanda! I know positions are really important to you and everything, but he'd be too restless to stay here.

PAUL: You can be restless anywhere. You can create it by staying terribly patient on top of the restlessness and by the sullen way you drag yourself around, but I want you to join the family and give attention to your mother.

JOHN: Well, why don't we ask Mother. Mother, do you feel you have my attention?

JOANNE: Enough to keep talking.

JOHN: See, I realize you want a three-shot and everything, but for him to separate himself is more logical, if you see what I'm saying. I just think it's better for people to pursue their objectives now, I mean if that's what you want—

The subject of the argument is trivial compared to what still needs to be accomplished this first afternoon, but the underlying issue is enormous: John's faintly provocative references to "three-shots" (i.e., three actors in the same camera shot) and "positions" suggest that it might seem to him that technical considerations supersede artistic ones in Paul's mind, and he is trying to see if he can give this director his trust. In addition, there seems to be a testing of opposing directorial views coming into the open: Paul's wish to include in his staging, even from the outset, the needs of the camera as the ultimate teller of the story, as opposed to what seems to be John's desire to be free to go anywhere while the camera has the obligation to find him. He seems to be saying that in no event should movements be choreographed on the actors so soon. The issue isn't fire escapes and smoking: it's an actor's request to be allowed unhampered creative investigation by a director who believes in it at least as much as he does, but is too scattered this afternoon to represent himself well. I have watched this hopeful day slide into confusion and I wonder why it is happening.

PAUL: Do it again.

Paul's voice is hoarse and he looks bone-tired. He sighs when he sees John go to stand in the doorway that leads to the fire escape. Karen, the strain of the morning's first reading behind her, is marvelous as Laura now, and very understanding of John's problem, practically willing him into the parlor with her eyes in order to give him the motivation he needs, then petting him in gratitude when he joins her on the two metal chairs that stand in for their couch. At each step of her silent invitation John resists, yielding finally only because she is the sister he loves and she wants him there, enduring only for her their mother's illusionary memories, then egging Amanda on in order to amuse himself, and finding to his horror, in the happy innocence of Joanne's response to him, a reason to love her.

PAUL: Well, okay, but I can't believe this whole scene is about Laura making Tom come in with her eyes.

I'm surprised when he sees no more value in it than that, but the smoking issue seems to be settled for the moment. I remember what Patricia Collinge, that great character actress and writer of wonderful satires, said to me once when I was having my own raging conflicts on a film: "But, Sonny, that's why you're in it! Don't you know everybody *hates* the joy of creation?"

Paul sits down beside Joanne while everyone else moves away, using the buffet with its Irish soda bread as a pretext for giving director and star their privacy. Across the room from them, pretending what I like to think of as blithe indifference, I uncoil my ear like a garden hose and send it over to eavesdrop, but it doesn't quite reach. Paul listens to her attentively, eyes narrowed, head back, arms crossed, while she bashes away at some notion with closed fists. In the middle of it he lets go that deep unearthly rumble he acquired from a dromedary on *The Silver Chalice,* the sound I call his "camel groan," but she goes on talking, hands flying like leaves now, and I wish I could hear what point she is making. Her plainspokenness with him always amazes me: she never holds back, never censors herself, is the only one who won't coddle him, and so he trusts her completely. She is more independent of him than he is of her and respects him enough to tell him the unvarnished truth as she sees it, even with the difficulties he is having with himself today. She never makes him wrong, never embarrasses him, and along with her truth goes an implied promise to let go of it if he can prove to her a better way. Paul, whatever the pressure, is seldom unkind and never mean. He is, at work, the same patient democrat he strives to be in life, of spacious tolerance but ever the figure of authority, simply because of who he is as a man and what he knows. As a director, his search is only for the way that works; there is no vanity in it, nothing to hide.

Six o'clock arrives like a kiss of forgiveness. Paul rises stiffly, as if he had spent the whole day wrestling with eels. Joanne calls out a good-night as she packs up her bag:

JOANNE: Wasn't this fun? Five actors, three of us directors, and each with sixteen different ideas of the way it should go!

Paul, Joanne, and I are taken in silence across the Triborough Bridge by one of the Teamster drivers, a heavyset, fatherly ex-cop who will let them off at their apartment on upper Fifth Avenue, then drop me off for dinner at my mother's. Paul is depressed and I don't know what to say. The silence goes on so long, the driver clears his throat.

STEWART: So what did you think of Malkovich today?

PAUL: Remind me to keep his mustache until he's photographed.

STEWART: Photographed for what?

PAUL: The picture.

STEWART: What picture?

PAUL: On the wall.

JOANNE: The one of his father. Who "fell in love with long distance."

She is still knitting what appears to be the same row she has been laboring over all day. She asks, "Will the father be in uniform, the way he is in the play?" Paul says no, he wants him in a straw boater and a bow tie, dapper and jaunty; he wants him to look like a "swinger of his time." There is another long silence.

PAUL: It was disastrous. I can say with absolute certainty that I certainly was uncertain.

JOANNE: Oh, the first day's always a mess!

PAUL: It's not just first-day uncertainty. I was aimless and I don't know why. I hate aimlessness.

JOANNE: It's all just happening at once, that's all. It can't possibly be like a normal first rehearsal. We've all done this play before, here and there.

Because I can't help him, I wish the ride would end. I keep remembering the way he spoke in that loud unnatural voice, without looking at anyone or seeing whether anyone was looking at him, as though he were addressing some large congregation of strangers instead of four uncertain actors, not a dozen feet away, one of whom happened to be his wife. We arrive at their apartment house and they go inside, he without saying good night—a bit bowed and carrying his briefcase—and she still sprightly under her burden of knitting, books, and all her unanswered mail. They want only to walk their dog, lock their door, and climb into bed. I watch them disappear into the lobby, then we drive on. As Paul himself has put it on other occasions, "Well, a not uninteresting day."

Second Day of Rehearsal

Our gray dungeon is silent when I come in, late. Mary sits by herself in a corner, storing up calm. Paul, his eyes invisible behind dark glasses, tilts backward on a metal chair, his hands behind his head. Joanne and Karen, the only actors scheduled for this morning, face him. He had evidently been speaking, then stopped when I came in, and they are waiting for him to begin again. In the lull, Joanne pulls out her knitting but stows it again immediately when she sees it bothers him. I tiptoe to a chair, mouthing "Good morning," and quietly take my seat.

PAUL: I apologize for yesterday. At four o'clock this morning I thought, It's really interesting. Yesterday was a study in uncertainty, a revelation in disparities, and I didn't know why. I was concerned with getting you up on your feet, trying to anticipate the camera, settling things. And what I really have to settle is where the hell all of us are, and what our beginning should be. It's so deceptive: the two of you, and Jim Naughton, have been doing the play all summer and you're giving a completely realized performance—for the stage. You have investigated the impulses—for the stage. Blocked the movements—for the stage. And on the one hand I'm seduced by that into doing what I did yesterday, accepting the stage performance and simply polishing it. Bringing down the scale of it a little. Adjusting the blocking a little. And letting it go. But on the other hand there's John—on a completely different rung of the ladder. He's done it for the stage, too, but long ago, in a different place, with different people and a different point of view. He needs to find his way into this family, and since he's a different son and brother, so do you. How do we make one family out of you? Do I simply ignore the disparities and try to smooth you all together around impulses you discovered for the stage in two completely unrelated productions? Simply go ahead and block as though the disparities weren't there? Or do I stop everything and ask you to disassemble everything you've done and begin from scratch, let you investigate each other from scratch, find new impulses together in the context of your being a different family now that John is here? Nothing's the same for you: different circumstances, different personalities, different medium—

JOANNE: Different home—all those rooms!

KAREN: Different everything!

PAUL: So should I do that? Forget the camera and all the other technical considerations for now and unleash you all to explore, as though you'd never played it?

KAREN: Let's explore. Let's explore our home, you want to?

The prospect delights and relieves Joanne. The women rise and begin to walk the tape-marked floor like suburban brides out house hunting, exclaiming over all those things they never had onstage as they come to them: the hallway, the kitchen, a real bedroom for Amanda, a pantry for Tom to sleep in! *"Wha-a-t?"* cries Joanne in a voice like Edith Bunker's. "He sleeps in a *p-a-a-ntry?"* Paul scratches his head and grins: this isn't precisely what he had in mind when he said "explore," but on they go, conjuring up everything in the place as they pass through: where windows are, the typing table, the phonograph, where plants will hang, where napkin rings are stored. And as she describes aloud each piece of imagined furniture inside these imagined walls, dredging up out of her childhood remembered things and making them real before her inner eye, Joanne's accent grows richer and her hands begin to move in a different way. Paul notes that, taking it as a sign that she has reached a deeper plane. Karen, lurching from room to room on that frozen knee she's invented for Laura's limp, leads Joanne the way a delighted child might do, following party ribbons to a hidden prize.

KAREN: Are we in front of the fireplace now?

JOANNE: I think we're *in* it!

They shriek with laughter and fall on each other's necks while Paul watches them, at once amused and bemused.

PAUL: When I said "explore" I didn't mean it quite that literally.

JOANNE [*laughing as she looks at the empty room and takes up her knitting*]: Well, we had a fine trip and I thought it was wonderful. Now I know where everything is.

Paul stands leaning on his shepherd's crook, biting the inside of his lip, which helps him think.

PAUL: Joanne! Remember "Pinch it"?

JOANNE: What! Not that old thing!

PAUL: Not *old* thing, *new* thing. Not character this time. Scale. You've got to pinch down the scale.

"Pinch it" is an echo of *Rachel, Rachel*—where the phrase became their code word. It was Paul's constant reminder to Joanne that the shy schoolteacher she portrayed had to smile a pinched, turned-down smile, that her pinched words had to be placed like separate seeds beyond the barriers of her lips, that her pinched toes had to be turned in, and her pinched enjoyment hidden. During the course of the filming the reminder to "pinch it" had been distilled still further, until it was only a tiny wordless gesture of pinching.

PAUL: So when I say "Pinch it" this time, it'll just mean "Take it down."

JOANNE: If you want me to act just give me the props and point me in the right direction. [*with a leer, to Karen*] I'm a prop actress, you see.

Karen laughs. Paul asks Mary Bailey for yesterday's notes and he takes scraps of things from his pockets, on which he has written others in the night.

PAUL: Karen. About yesterday. I liked Laura's acceptance, but use it more sparingly. If she seems too serene we can lose the sense that she's crippled.

KAREN: I think the real crippling, the emotional crippling, happened later. After the play. After her brother left. What I need to do is find ways to let people know it's going to happen.

PAUL: Aha! Telegraph poles!

KAREN: But you said "too serene"—

PAUL: Not if you linger on it when it's not appropriate. That will make you truly eccentric. That's one telegraph pole. Too *much* acceptance, too *much* serenity are as much signs of illness as "Help!" is. What I'm looking for is imbalance. Jangled gears. I don't care what the imbalance is as long as it's there. She could spend too long polishing silver. Stare at lint on her finger too long. Concentrate too hard on what shouldn't need concentration at all. Doesn't matter. Surprise me. Keep me off-balance too.

He finds what looks like a bus transfer in his pocket and reads the back of it.

PAUL: Ahahah! "The Limp!" Fine for the stage, but too big for film. Just curl your toes inside your shoe and walk on the outside of your foot. That'll be enough. Don't even let me see it. The impulse is fine in what you're doing—it's only a question of size.

He rubs his hands briskly, then claps them.

All right, the Deception scene! Let's just do it. Karen, do something at the beginning, some activity. Be polishing the animals. Look out the window and see your mother coming. Run and hide what you've been doing. Or you could be listening to your records and hear your mother over them. Up to you.

KAREN: Well, for the time being I'm just going to be right here on the floor.

She sits there, pretending a book is the glass menagerie, dreaming and humming to herself until Joanne stamps to indicate that she has opened the door. Karen flees to her typewriter. Joanne enters, so involved in her character and the goal of the scene, so consumed with the feelings she has given herself to come in with, that she forgets her line. But she doesn't let it throw her, never drops Amanda: she stands for a moment with an expression of such complexity, betrayal, bewilderment, defeat, and broken hope that when, weeks from now, she repeats it on film at Paul's request, it will be his favorite close-up in the picture. Being a conscious actress as well as an intuitive one, and having arrived at this moment once, Joanne will be able to resurrect it whenever it's needed, always coming to it freshly by a different road. She breaks it now by suddenly scratching her nose.

JOANNE: Honey, since we're not stuck in our old stage positions, couldn't I yank off my gloves and throw them down when I say, "Deception! Deception!" and then just run over and tear up her typing?

That she can break so quickly from an image dredged from a primal place, and then dispose of it with the scratch of an itchy nose, simply astounds him, and his delight in her is too full to let him reply. "What?" she asks, smiling a little, pretending not to understand why he stands there so mutely, but he only shakes his head.

They run through the scene again. He listens with his chin on his shepherd's crook, sunglasses hanging from an ear. Anxiety makes Laura shudder like a victim of third-degree burns when Amanda searches bloody-handed through the entrails of the future, a priestess reading the signs of the terrible dependency into which they will sink as a result of Laura's deceitful truancy from typing school. I know that Joanne must be drawing on her own Depression childhood, when she cared for the pretty mother who was always a child to her. She sighs to the bottom of her soul as the terrible visions arise, then releases them completely to chirp about the wonders charm can do, and when she sees her wayward husband's picture on the wall, she gives it the old fungoo and we all collapse. Paul springs between Joanne and Karen, light as Puck.

PAUL: Here's what it is then! This! And this!

He floats his hands toward each other through the air, toward and away, toward and away, like two magnetized Swiss kissing dolls whose lips attract and repel.

PAUL: It's contact, no contact. Contact, no contact. Coming together, drifting apart. Your closeness as you both see into the future is excellent. But that first beat, when Joanne's moving in on you—

KAREN: Right! No closeness. Hide in my typing.

PAUL: Shuffle your papers. Anything.

KAREN [*excited*]: Like a deck of cards, yes! I want to hide—

PAUL [*shouting*]: Do, but then don't. You're off-balance.

KAREN: I play with my hair—

JOANNE: She can't even *hear* me.

KAREN: I don't *want* to hear you!

JOANNE [*practical suddenly*]: I have to cross so far to reach that typewriter. Can't I attack something from here?

PAUL: Sure, you can throw things as far as you can. Your coat, your hat, your scarf, your gloves, throw them all! Little attacks—

JOANNE: Till I feel the big one coming on.

PAUL: Keep throwing till you *have* to cross to that typewriter.

JOANNE: I rip the page out, come back and throw some more.

KAREN: What if she catches me before I get there? Do I freeze the way children do? I'm guilty. I turn invisible.

JOANNE: And the glass menagerie is everywhere! All over the room, not just one place. Can't it be everywhere?

The ideas tossed among them conjure a nineteenth-century scene: battledore and shuttlecock—a youth with his maidens on a lawn backlighted in the spray of fountains, nimble, lovely, light. Paul lifts a hand. Tableau. Another game.

PAUL: Go back. Start again, but play it for seventy-two seconds *without* starting. Let's just develop "getting caught." Karen, what's your first line?

KAREN: "Hello, Mother. I was just—"

PAUL: That's all? "I was just—"? Broken off like that? Good! Say it just that way. Give me a minute and a half of the scene without either of you saying anything, then give me "I was just—"

As I help Paul shove the blue couch to where the window seat will be, Joanne warns him, as a reminder that his ribs are broken, "You're never going to race this weekend if you keep moving heavy things around." Karen lies down on the couch, diddling a little horse she has fashioned in the last few minutes of some foil from Paul's sandwich. Pretending it's glass, she holds it up to the light, then freezes when she sees Amanda already in the room. Joanne, furious, mimes tearing off her coat. Karen sits up quickly, shrinking into herself, submissive, frightened, still. Then very slyly, in full view of Joanne, she edges over to the typewriter and pretends to have been there all the time. "Hello, Mother. I was just—" There is something inappropriate and insane about the timing: the first of the "telegraph poles." A minute and a half has gone by. Then, hat, coat, gloves thrown, "Deception! Deception!" comes from Joanne like the steam of a geyser and propels her to the typewriter in such a boiling rage that only the action of ripping the paper from it and hurling it across the room saves Laura from physical attack. This interpretation is new territory for Joanne and she flings herself into its exploration as recklessly as a dancer, giving up all that had worked for her on the stage in order to break into discoveries that could never be found unless she was willing to risk being clumsy, embarrassed, forgetful of lines, a fool in front of everyone.

Paul watches with that disassembled face that seems reserved only for her, then tells her to try a "Kazan transition" while still in the midst of worrying about the fifty dollars Amanda has wasted on Laura's tuition so she will be ready to cry, "Don't turn on that phonograph!" at the instant Laura escapes to it.

PAUL [*jumping up and down, shaking his fist*]: Do not, do not, do not, do not, *do not turn on that phonograph!*

Joanne gives him a look and says, rather dryly, that she gets the point. Paul takes his sunglasses off the ear they've been hanging on and shoves them back onto his nose. He takes a golf swing with his shepherd's crook, hooks it over his shoulder, and forgets it. The scene continues: deprived now of her phonograph and the comfort of old records, Karen skitters past Joanne to the sanctuary of the glass menagerie.

JOANNE: My God! She leaves me alone to go to *that?* I think, "What's she doing? I don't know what she's *doing* with those little glass animals!" Then I realize they're her refuge to escape to from *me!*

PAUL: Good, Karen. Only go there in your head before you walk there. Now it looks as if a director said, "Walk," so you're walking. And do the moment backward when you leave Joanne. Attack her with a line that's not an attack line. Do everything backward. It's fine!

And out of this scene of deception comes a healing between mother and daughter. Laura's revelation of her high school love for a boy named Jim O'Connor combines with Amanda's hope that a man might appear one day to save them, to create one of the tenderest moments of the play, when, in denying Laura's handicap, Amanda demonstrates for her how charming "a slight defect" can be, how gracefully one can conceal a limp beneath a long, sashaying skirt as it whisks across a ballroom floor. "When you've got a slight disadvantage like that, you've just got to cultivate something else to take its place. You have to cultivate charm—or vivacity—or charm!" Joanne cries, limping and waltzing before Karen like a plover hen teaching a fledgling how to feign a broken wing, then stopping suddenly under her husband's picture, craning to it nearly on tiptoe, remembering their long-ago obsession, eyes eager and alight, a girl again. "That's the only thing your father had plenty of—charm!" Then the eagerness collapses and Joanne subsides, like something dying, into the workworn bones of Amanda. The scene ends. No one moves. Paul clears his throat to bring us back to reality. Then he calls a short break.

I watch Mary Bailey, whom I am growing to love. She is so like Joanne's character in *Rachel, Rachel*—physically very self-conscious, and so empathic she seems to have been born without a skin. Her expression now is a little woeful as she samples her way along the buffet, pretending great disinterest in what it offers, keeping her chewing tiny and secret, then, when the break is over, picking up her clipboard again to take her devotion back to Paul. She is the complete professional and he adores her for it and has whispered to me twice that she's the best he's had at the job. I think her fragility is part illusion because nothing except injustice seems to crack her. She likes herself.

PAUL: Okay, guys, here's where we lock it in cement. Just say the lines so Mary can hear. Don't play it—walk it.

Mary watches closely, taking careful notes of every move so they can repeat the choreography later. Then morning rehearsal ends. Joanne dances a series of mock curtsies that carry her backward across the floor. Paul signals "Pinch it!" and she laughs at that and goes to him, feeling his face, here, there, there, as though checking him for fever.

PAUL: Well, I feel better than yesterday.

JOANNE: Aw! You didn't feel good yesterday?

PAUL: I thought we were going in circles yesterday.

JOANNE: That's okay. Going in circles doesn't hurt.

She holds him a moment to rub his head, then prances off with Karen to look for a knitting shop. Paul orders his half a tuna sandwich. Michael comes to him, full of ideas from having watched the scene. He wants to start with a low-angle upshot of the glass animal in Karen's hand, freeze on it at the sound of Joanne's key in the lock, then go to Karen's startled eyes. Paul admires many of Michael's ideas but likes his process even more: his enthusiasm, his loyalty, and his dogged willingness, when the two men disagree, to keep climbing back into the ring for another round.

They all leave Paul alone for the lunch hour. He lies on the old couch resting and studying his script in this antiquated place that smells so much like a gym, with its ticking pipes breaking the silence. He is preparing for John. I sit just beyond his sight line, being quiet, watching him. I think he must be one of the very few on earth not impressed by the fact that he is the only Paul Newman people think of when they hear that name, the source from which that giant image comes, reproduced in theatres everywhere for nearly forty years, part of our consciousness, our vocabulary, the original die, the only one of him, lying here a foot away. I wonder how that feels. Watching his eyelids begin to lower, watching him breathe, with his ribs broken, and his sinuses stuffed, and his raging throat and everything in his head on overload, all I can see is my friend— my hard-working, worrying, gray-headed friend, who was boning up for his meeting with John the way he must have crammed for exams at Kenyon, until moments ago when he finally fell asleep.

*   *   *

John Malkovich, sensitive to the quiet in the room, comes in as stealthily as Peter Pan slipping over the rail of the pirate ship, all eyes. He is dressed today in expensive baggy tweeds, with an ever-wrinkle shirt, a vest sweater, and a money belt. The little blond curlicue pigtail is still in place. I think of what Béjart called his ballet about Nijinsky, *Clown of God,* and that's what Malkovich may be. I've known very few. They're like freak hailstones that melt before you can show them to your friends. Brando is one. Paul yawns mightily, bestirring himself, and suddenly notices John.

JOHN [*putting his things down*]: I hear you've had a revelation.

PAUL: A minor revelation.

JOHN: Oh, just minor.

PAUL: About what was going on yesterday. Yah.

As the other actors start drifting back from lunch, Paul withdraws with John to a corner and repeats what he said to Joanne and Karen this morning. As John listens, I see immediate agreement in his eyes. It doesn't take much explaining.

PAUL: I'm not going to flog it to death, I just thought it was interesting. Which brings us to this afternoon. [*He calls to the rest of the room.*] Guys? Let's do the Quarrel scene.

In spite of John's petition yesterday, with Joanne's ardent support, that the Quarrel scene start in the middle as it does in the first published version of the play, Paul decides to stay with the later one where clear provocation for the fight has been provided by Amanda fussing at Tom not to write in the dark, and to "sit up straight" to save his "poor little heart." But having made the decision, Paul broods, leaning on his shepherd's crook and frowning over how to begin. The actors circle him in silence, blowing on hot drinks and frowning too, as if by taking on his expression they could share his load. Their circling takes John to the parlor.

JOHN: Uh—is this the typewriter I use, or just Laura's? Or do I write longhand?

PAUL [*staring holes into the floor*]: Longhand.

JOHN: That's what I thought, too.

Paul wrestles with a footnote in his script where the playwright decrees that "Tom and Amanda remain in the dining room throughout their argument." Despite the fact that this is film, and film invites opening up, Paul is mindful of his promise to render Tennessee Williams "pure," so he won't make grand departures without good reason.

PAUL: But it's senseless. Tom's a sitting duck if he stays in this dining room! Why would he work in here when he knows he'll be persecuted here? The obligation of the scene isn't to a dining room—it's to create a situation that whips him into an absolute frenzy and drives him out of the house! It's Amanda's hovering, her constant hovering, even if it's meant as reverent caring, and the terrible sense of invasion that drive him out.

He suggests Tom's room as his starting place of choice, a set never seen in the play. For Amanda to encroach on him there, in his only sanctum, would heighten the sense of invasion enormously. Tony Walton has designed Tom's room as a converted pantry, opening off the hall beyond the kitchen, and just across from Amanda's bedroom door. The model represents it as a dark hole of horizontal wainscoting, narrow, high, and windowless, a cell of the condemned in the hold of a convict ship with a tiny desk and Tom's lonely cot at the bottom. But it has been designed without the "wild walls" usually provided that slide away to allow for camera movement in areas that are too confined. Michael Ballhaus issues a warning: in that room he will only be able to shoot from the waist up, mediums, cross angles, close-ups—talking heads! To shoot much of the scene in there would prove static and uncinematic. Paul thinks it's too early for concerns like that: actors' impulses must be considered first, then who knows where the scene might lead them? We follow him down the tapes marked "Hall" to Tom's room, where he invites the actors to "just feel your way." Joanne thinks Amanda should just happen to be passing Tom's door at the start of the scene, on her way to the parlor with her cup of bedtime tea. John sits at his "desk" and buries himself in the poem he is writing, then announces that he wants to wear reading glasses. Round ones. Mary writes down his request.

PAUL: She really comes in to say good night to him, Joanne, but she just can't resist giving him a little good-night zetz.

JOANNE: Zetz?

PAUL: Zutz?

Joanne repeats her walk down the hall but this time goes by John's door completely before tiptoeing back for just one tiny little peek. She admires him at his writing for a moment, then whispers his name from the door: "Tom?" It's not in the script, but it makes John snap "Shh!" at her as he tries to keep his concentration on his poem. This only invites her in, motivates her to fuss with his reading light, to worry about his eyes. Perfect.

But John stops the scene. He takes out the first published version of the play and shows Paul a passage from a section further on, where Amanda nags at Tom to comb his hair because he looks "so pretty" with his hair combed. John suggests that Paul pirate the passage and use it here instead of the reference to the reading light. Paul sees value in the suggestion: it might let Joanne become more physically involved, give her an excuse to push at Tom's hair before she pushes at his shoulders to sit up straight, and so drive him that much wilder. In the process of trying it John discovers wonderful business of his own to mock her with: he pretends to admire himself in a "mirror" while she straightens his hair, and discovers that he really *is* pretty! And when she pokes at his shoulders he braces himself like a good West Point cadet. Pretty boy. Model soldier. Anything she wants! And it's no surprise that he chooses to jump away from her, crying out, "What in Christ's name am I supposed to do!"—the first true opening blow of the fight. Paul is pleased. Stage performances are being let go of in this careful, moment-to-moment investigation, making room to discover the "life of the film." Tom has jumped away, but now what? What keeps him here to fight on? Why doesn't he just bang out of the house and forget the rest of the scene?

JOANNE: Maybe he can't. Maybe he's in his pajamas.

PAUL: His pajamas. Fine. The whole scene's about having to get dressed to get out of there.

JOHN [*grabbing a shirt*]: I think I want to brush my teeth. Does the sink work in the kitchen?

PAUL: Do it! Oh, that's good, grab your pants! Follow him,

Joanne. That's great! Into the kitchen. Up and down the hall. Keep bouncing from room to room.

It's volleyball this time, not battledore and shuttlecock, with Paul barking instructions like a coach. Joanne pads breathlessly after John as he ricochets in crazy flight from pantry to kitchen to hall, pantomiming as he goes the tearing off and yanking on of clothes.

PAUL: When you're done with your teeth smell your armpits. They're awful! Go back to the sink.

JOANNE [*out of breath*]: I don't know where I am. What am I doing?

PAUL: Following him. Keep following. Don't worry about it. She's a follower in this scene. John! Get caught in your turtleneck! Let him keep flapping half in and half out with that furious voice coming out of it!

It's a mess, but a lively mess, and a much better opportunity for the camera than Michael Ballhaus had feared. The scene winds down, drained of energy and ideas.

PAUL: Lots of options there.

JOHN: The time I'd like to brush my teeth is when she's saying she thinks I'm doing something I'm ashamed of when I say, "I go to the movies." It's a way to feel clean.

PAUL: Fine. Get rid of all the garbage in your mouth, brush it out while she's talking about it, then turn to her with a mouth full of foam. Just nifty! Let's do it! Show me!

They go back to the beginning, trying to remember where

they were, and Mary Bailey, erasing old positions in her script and scribbling in new ones till the page is as frayed as a failed math exam, somehow keeps track of it all. They repeat the scene and there are more surprises: on impulse, Joanne suddenly stops following and marches out of Tom's room, refusing to discuss with him a moment longer the filth he brings home from the public library, like "that hideous book by that insane Mr. Lawrence," and John must reverse his pattern by following her now, chasing her to her bedroom door for more of the argument, then ending it (he thinks) by slamming the door in her face, shouting, "I'm going out! Out! Out!" He slams his own door behind him as he goes into his room to dress, but Joanne, furious at his exclusion and the follower again, bursts in on him to continue her harassment till his shoes are on and he is fleeing her down the hall and into the parlor.

Here everyone stops to discuss the final beat of the scene, in which Tom turns into a scalded cat to attack her with what is traditionally the great comic aria of the play, the "I'm going to opium dens" speech.

JOHN: The way I see it, he's a raging little boy. I think it's all emotion, he's completely out of control. I think that's funnier.

John shares a horror story out of his childhood, how as a child of nine, yearning to enter the costume contest at the Halloween party at school, he found he had grown so big that nothing would fit him. He had begun to have "a kind of nervous breakdown about it" when his father came to his rescue. He wrapped John in a sheet, painted a single eye on his forehead, and sent him to school as the Cyclops, with a promise of certain victory. But his sister won, in a fairy dress from the dime store. And John, his pride undone, betrayed and crushed with grief, ran home and tore up the house. Tore it up so thoroughly, and so embarrassed himself by his tantrum, that all he could do was continue.

JOHN: So it's not really what he says—it's the torrent of emotion that's so funny. And so sad that she can't even cope with it.

PAUL: Show me.

JOHN: Because in 1944 it was probably shocking when he was raving about opium dens, and berating this poor little mother with the string of cathouses he says he's running, but today you need a different bead on that—!

PAUL: Show me.

JOHN: See, I *like* her! I mean she makes *demands* on her children. She doesn't teach them corner-cutting the way Willy Loman did. She's trying to teach *superior* things—at least, *she* thinks they're superior. And the speech comes from his shame at having a tantrum he can't stop, and whenever he tries to stop, it just gets worse.

PAUL: Show me.

John does—and he doesn't. It is raw abuse and hysteria, yet there are glimpses, too, of an authentic soul, but a soul so choked off and frustrated that no reasonable channels remain to it. I am surprised when Paul doesn't react. His only comment about what John has done concerns the tag of the scene: whether, as in the script, Tom should collide with the glass menagerie on his way out the door and stop to pick up the pieces, as John just did, or cut out the moment entirely, as Paul suggests. "Every guy who comes into this house breaks a glass animal!" Paul comments. John argues for the values he sees in doing it as written: Tom's awful recognition that in his fury at Amanda he might also have hurt his sister, and the chance to play on his knees, in the posture of a penitent, the great remorse he feels. But Paul says it raises too many questions: Why wouldn't Laura be gluing broken animals at the beginning of the next scene? And wouldn't Tom be obligated to comfort her after such a fiasco? And if he did, what would that do to his exit?

PAUL: So I'd like to end with "You ugly, babbling old witch!" And then bam! He's out! It's clean.

JOHN: I think he needs a moment of contrition.

PAUL: Show me. I-will-watch-and-I-will-listen-and-I-will-give-it-a-fair-try-but-I-will-not-love-it!

John demonstrates what he means, but Paul stands fast. They hear each other, but neither man will be persuaded by the other's reasons. Deadlock. Silence.

JOANNE: God, I wish I had a corset to rehearse in!

She wipes a snow pea through a poisonous-looking dip and bears it to me: "Try this marvelous taste." But I spurn it and she crunches it up herself, then turns to Paul. "Honey, do you think she wears glasses? Amanda? Sometimes?" But the Quarrel scene is chattering in his head and he walks right by her to pour himself some coffee. She goes to take up her knitting. John relaxes.

JOANNE: I'd like to start the scene in my bedroom and be putting on cold cream. I'd love that. Pond's. Or what was that stuff you put on after you'd wiped the cold cream off?

Night cream! I'm going to be putting on night cream and I'm going to pat my chin. Pat! Pat! I'll do my whole night routine. And have an old rag tied around my head.

PAUL: Let's give the whole scene another whack and just go through it slowly. Do you want to really play it or just figure out how to get the clothes on and off?

JOANNE: Just a minute! I'll drop a whole row!

Paul waits while she hurries her knitting, a needle clenched in her teeth like a pirate dagger. He stands shifting from foot to foot as her needles click, finally letting his shepherd's crook fall with a clatter that makes her look up. He is glaring down at her through one popped eye, like William Powell in *Life with Father,* a tower of haughty injury.

PAUL: I think you *may* be taking advantage of our relationship.

She puts her knitting away, picks up her script, and rises.

PAUL: So! Where's Laura during this fight?

KAREN: Watching. I've retreated to my bed on the parlor couch.

PAUL: Stay there. At least I'll have some idea where to find you.

JOANNE [*moving to her starting position*]: I don't know about you-all, but I'm sort of loosely arranged. Not tightly arranged. We should all be loosely arranged at this stage.

JOHN: We're loosely arranged because we don't have anything real to work with. Once we have props, and rooms with real walls—

PAUL: John, don't worry about how the scene ends; we can leave the end to fool around with. I just want to be sure the beginning and middle are set.

JOANNE: Is it all marked down? Do we know where we are?

PAUL: Astoria.

Joanne sits at her imaginary dressing table and pretends to finish patting night cream on her face. Then she carries her make-believe tea past Tom's door, and it all starts again. But this time, as they search, they find more comfort, more humor, more of themselves. Joanne, heeding Paul's occasional reminders to "remember The Lady" when she prods at Tom, increasingly finds ways of making her intrusions on him the slightest, lightest, most delicate and flutelike demonstrations of maternal concern, what Paul calls her "reverent caring," and there is no way one could oppose them. Apart from those savage moments when they are flaying each other openly, her version of Tom's tormentor is always just beyond reach, a tireless, vulnerable, genteel mosquito whose feathery bite is the kiss that confounds and whose whine is the purr of true love. There is nothing here of that brutal, barking, harridan nagging I've seen in other performers that gives Tom such open season on his mother. He is defenseless against this Amanda: her loving attentions keep him so off-balance and ambivalent that all he can do with his rage is think it's wrong, lose it in ridiculous tantrums that leave him even more humiliated, or turn it viciously against himself. With every repetition of the scene it has found new iridescence, has elaborated itself into more and more intricate nuances, unfolding as a child's Japanese paper flower unfolds, upward through a glass of water from the clamshell that had concealed it.

But every time he reaches the climax, that awesome outburst about opium dens, John veers away from the drop that he could ride to the bottom of the hill.

Paul is satisfied that they have worked well and have found the impulses and moments in the scene, and believes that with nearly two weeks left to rehearse in, there will be plenty of time to polish. But there's a feeling of letdown in such accomplishment, and I think about going home until I realize with shock that it is barely half past four! They will have to wind themselves up all over again to break into a scene they haven't tried. Paul revs himself, briskly rubbing heat into his palms, like an overbooked masseur with one last client to face. He glances into Mary's script to see where he is.

PAUL: So! The Drunk scene. We could start it one of two ways: Karen, you're in bed, you hear something, you go to the door, and he simply falls into the room. Or, he's downstairs fumbling for a key he has dropped, singing "Bye, Bye, Birdie," and that's how you hear him.

JOHN [*quietly*]: I think it's "Blackbird." "Bye, Bye, Blackbird."

John takes himself to a strip of floor marked "Stairs," then falls to his hands and knees. Karen jumps up from the metal chair where she has been talking to Paul, pantomimes opening a door, and quietly calls, "Tom?" Paul laughs.

PAUL: No, no, no! Come back! We haven't even talked about it yet!

Karen and John come back and sit down.

PAUL: A word of caution. The scene is not about drunkenness. It's the only time we see Tom and Laura alone long enough to really seem like brother and sister, and if it serves to sort of "thicken" their relationship, the scene makes this an ensemble play and not just a series of star turns. The booze just helps us see the depth of his affection and despair for her, lets it come forth a little more boldly, but it should never seem to *come* from the booze. His sweetness and silliness do, and his hangover does the next morning, but booze is not the burden of the scene. So, John: loose, but not woggly-eyed.

JOHN: I think they're not just close, they're *unnaturally* close. I think this scene is where Tennessee had a chance to act out what made him write the play at all, to sort of exorcise the guilt he felt over leaving his sister Rose behind. And I think when Tom brings her the scarf—I know you won't like this, but I do—I think he brings it to her to apologize for knocking over her little glass animals.

PAUL: I never liked that and I think it raises problems. I'm not convinced that I'm going to let him do it.

JOHN [*going right past it*]: I don't mean "unnaturally close" as *sexually* close. Just that they spent every single minute of their childhood together because they were both so shy, and so sort of beleaguered by everything that was going on in the house.

PAUL: And I think falling down on the stairs may not be the best way to start the scene. What does a drunk do when he falls down, anyway?

JOANNE [*with a maniacal laugh from across the room*]: You should know!

PAUL: I think he's just looking for his key. He's got a little toy
noisemaker, one of those little cymbal things with clappers
on it, and that's what Laura hears.

John hasn't answered Paul and Paul hasn't answered John. It's
not really as though they hadn't heard each other: it's like a
circus act, two clowns who keep missing whenever they try to
shake hands. They start the scene.

When Karen catches him on the landing on hands and knees,
John turns to her the face of a little boy, with a half-guilty, half-
delighted smile spread across it. He lets her lead him up the
imaginary staircase the way a child would let a nanny help him
to a waiting tub after a nasty fall. And he speaks breathlessly as
a child would, saying each "a" in his ABC way: "There was *a*
Garbo picture—and *a* Mickey Mouse—and *a* travelogue. . . .
But the wonderfullest trick of all was the coffin trick." And
when, later on, he shouts, "Goody, goody! Pay 'er back for all
those Rise an' Shines," it sounds perfectly consistent with the
little boy he's playing. Finishing the run-through, he gives a
nod of little-boy approval to himself. It is a surprising choice,
charming in its innocence, and bold, a flashback to a time of
secrets shared, when a young brother could allow a little moth-
ering from his sister, and Karen has been with John all the way.
When the scene ends, Paul makes no reference to John's interpretation.

PAUL: Hmm. Well. The other thing is—[*as though he had
mentioned a* first *thing*]—Karen, what wakes you is that
noisemaker. He's fumbling around, looking for his key,
then he rises into your view like a Phoenix. "I have been to
the movies!" Ta-daa! And John. With the scarf: instead of
waving it as you come up the stairs, find a special place to
reveal it, then simply allow the magic to take place.

They run through it again but it seems mechanical. John, having dropped the "little boy" for want of encouragement, seems to have lost spirit. Paul suggests that he simply sit on the stairs with no plan to ascend them, alone, drunk, happy, and unaware of Laura. The actor obeys and they begin again. When he hears Karen approach, John wiggles his fingers at her without looking, backward over his head, and smiles an invitation for her to join him. It's nice but it's missing his heart. They try again.

PAUL: Turn the staircase into a mountain, John. Come one step, stop. Tell her one line of your adventure. Come another step, stop. Another line—

John does exactly as he's told, and it's as lifeless as it is cooperative. I know how Paul despises arbitrary "traffic cop" direction, and I can only guess that he imposes this on John because he thinks that a new physical pattern, no matter how arbitrary, might force him to wrench his inner process into a different channel and make him find an emotional alternative to the little boy Paul appears to dislike.

It seems to work, for midway in his "mountain climbing" John begins to experiment and finds "things up his sleeve." In fact he has hidden the scarf there, and for the next several minutes I am given a lesson in how an inventive actor invests an inert prop with life and, by shifting his attitude and concentration, excites himself:

He whisks the scarf out of his sleeve, surprising and delighting Karen, who didn't know it was there, and now waves it in Kabuki undulations over her head while enthralling her with his recitation of the marvelous transformations performed by Malvolio the Magician before his eyes.

It's hard not to break in with a thought of my own that John's discovery inspires: why not have Tom try to *transform* Laura with the scarf? Pray that it changes her into the sister he wishes she were—free, happy, the crippled leg healed—change her as Malvolio changed water into bourbon! But it fails! Pulling the scarf away and finding her still the same, he would present the bit of silk to her as the dead souvenir of dead hope. I tell Paul about it later, and he tells John, who doesn't do it. But when I see the movie I think it's there.

PAUL: Good! This time, John, don't show her the scarf all at once. Forget where you put it. Search in all your pockets, like an after-dinner speaker who's lost his notes, then find it and inch it out slowly. Tantalize her. Make her take it from you. Then Karen! Spellbind him with it. Use it to lure him back to the apartment.

John stops on his way "upstairs" and suddenly places a hand on Karen's forehead in a gesture of anguished benediction whose tenderness and eloquence pierce me, but he never repeats it again. Paul lets the scene rest where it is, confident that these actors are so rich in impulses that when filming starts the set itself will instruct them in whatever technical adjustments need to be made. What no one can anticipate now is how marvelous a teacher that set will prove itself, and how, through an accident of mistiming, it will lift the scene to a level of extraordinary intimacy and revelation. Five-thirty has come.

PAUL: Shall we do the "Mommy, I'm Sorry" scene?*

JOANNE [*still knitting*]: Oh, it's such a biggie, and those fluorescent lights just make me want to sleep. I need a nap.

* The Apology scene—see Appendix.

She lays down her knitting, unhinges her jaw with both hands, and yawns prodigiously. Paul decides to call it a day. "That's a wrap!" he says, but Joanne has wandered to the buffet.

JOANNE: I'm going to take everything on this table home and make an enormous bread pudding. Oh, look! Doughnut holes! I never even saw those. [*Daintily, she samples one.*] No, not for the pudding. Too sweet.

Nevertheless, she polishes it off, then eats a carrot to restore her virtue and departs in a flurry of good-nights. I ascend alone from our flickering dungeon to the street above. The darkness I meet there astounds me, for I have had no window through which to see night arrive. I ride the free jitney back to Manhattan. The city throbs and sparkles under a purple sky. I dine on take-out chicken, ordering twice what I can eat, and eat it all, in an orgy of loneliness. I'm too tired to phone anyone to tell them I'm in town. At midnight I call my wife—my gift to myself for the day.

Third
Day of
Rehearsal

Paul strides in, sunny in a yellow shirt and fresh as spring's first crocus. Joanne comes like a crowd, spreading warm greetings and the news of the world. She stops to see how Karen's knitting is coming along, yards and yards of something soft and beautiful, remarkable colors and patterns. And over by the coffee urn John is treating his old friend Michael Ballhaus like the honoree at a Friar's Club Roast, with a teasing that never seems to stop and that Michael receives with unwavering beams of affection. Paul wants to get to work on the "Mommy, I'm Sorry" scene, the most difficult one in the play, heavy with exposition, blunted in its thrust by the fitful starts of multiple confrontations, and offering no clear hints for a pattern of physical movement. Five pages long in the script, the sequence will time at over thirteen minutes on the screen and, with the exception of the Gentleman Caller scene, will take longer to rehearse than any other.

After his tirade about opium dens, and his drunken return

with the magic scarf, Tom has awakened with a hangover. He and his mother drink their coffee in silence while Amanda waits for him to say he's sorry. When he does, she reveals only gradually her reason for sending Laura to the store and for confronting him: Tom must not abandon his sister as his father abandoned them all! Amanda suspects he intends to do so after finding among his things a letter of acceptance from the Merchant Marine, to which, secretly, he has applied. Whatever Tom does, he must see that Laura is provided for before he goes. Caught, guilty, and furious, he can only shout his agreement when Amanda badgers him to bring home a gentleman caller for his sister.

They sit in a circle mulling over the scene. Karen is knitting. Joanne sips tea from a Styrofoam cup. John lounges against a table, a dozen feet away.

PAUL: Joanne, let's examine what Amanda's really doing at the beginning of this. She's in the living room, lying in wait for him—

JOHN: Why wouldn't she lie in wait in the dining room? That's where they always have coffee.

PAUL: I think today she'd have coffee in the living room, just to keep him from going out the door when he hears what she's got to say.

JOHN: But it's not just coffee. It's cereal too. I mean, she sets the table every day, and I think having to sit where they always sit, but not be able to say anything, would have a lot more tension.

The play's directions state that the scene occurs in the living room. The oddness of that, of Amanda having to balance Tom's shredded wheat on a tiny end table, just to cut off avenues of escape, appeals to me. To my surprise, Paul doesn't argue for his view; he lets it go. They adjourn to the dining room as John suggests, and Paul says, "Let's begin."

"Let's begin." No one who is not an actor can imagine the terror in those words: to have to stand exposed again no matter how prepared you are or how much "technique" you have, to have to open your mouth and speak, not knowing how you will sound or look! No past success reassures you, if you can even recall one, only faith, the courage to be a fool, and the hope that your director is skilled enough to catch you when you fall. Joanne's expression shifts: she's Amanda again.

She stands sipping coffee across the table from where John is having his. A long silence, full of awareness. Then, very cautiously, as though she were reaching through iron bars to offer a wild elephant a handful of hay, Joanne pretends to push a coffeepot just within Tom's reach, then backs quickly away with a sigh. Their glances brush, then fly apart. Another silence. You can almost hear the pulses in their ears. At last he mutters his apology, so softly she can barely guess what he said, but it's enough to overwhelm her with relief. The scene becomes too intimate to hear. I can read the scene on Paul's face, and Joanne's gray curls, bobbing up and down for emphasis, tell me she is warning John that "too-hot drinks makes cancer of the stomach" and is urging upon him the healing benefits of cream. The scene tacks this way and that for a while, propelled by a very faint breeze, while Paul stands holding his forehead. When it ends, with Joanne's scuttling pursuit of John to the door, fussing at him to put on his scarf, clinging to his lapels as he wheels and spins like some hair-raising carnival ride, pleading with him to bring home that gentleman caller—"Honey, will you? Will you? Will you?"—Paul finally smiles. But Michael Ballhaus isn't smiling at all; he is looking at his watch.

MICHAEL: Do you know how many minutes they sit at that table?

PAUL: What do you think, John?

JOHN: I think it works fine at the table. The tension holds. I mean as an actor—speaking for myself—but that's how I feel.

PAUL: It all happens too easily. Not enough roadblocks. Violate the intentions. Joanne! Give him the advantage, pour him more coffee, hover, wait and see what he'll do. But John, no matter what the script says, refuse to apologize. Just finish your coffee and get up and go. I want to see the effort it takes to do that, to leave without saying you're sorry. And you see you're getting nowhere, Joanne. It's not going to happen. Just lose the battle. Then let's see what he does.

JOANNE: I'd never stay there. I'd go straight to my room.

PAUL: Do it. Show me.

This time when Joanne pretends to pour his cereal, coolly solicitous even while her wounds still fester, John suddenly excludes her from his life by including her in a dead glance that offers no hope. The deliberate calm with which he blows on his coffee while he studies her reveals the dangerous game with which he's exciting himself: "What if I don't apologize? What if I just walk out and never see her again?" He stretches the pleasure in the thought by slowly toying with his cup. Joanne, sitting opposite, yearns across the table for the words that would end this impasse, but keeps her attention on her own cup, where she has hidden all her feelings and her pride. John plays with her, clicking his cup with a fingernail as if considering a change of heart, then he bangs it onto the floor decisively and quickly ties his shoe. Joanne gives a grim little nod of acceptance, rises primly, girds herself in the armor of dignity, and goes to her room. She sits at her "dressing table," her back to the door. At her exit, John's game collapses. The man who would escape becomes the boy again, who must drag himself shyly to his mother's door and say he's sorry in a voice that doesn't trust itself to speak. No other way out. Joanne, borne high now on the dreadful seesaw of their game, continues to sit there, perfectly still, grateful for the miracle of his remorse; then, with all her mother's guilt welling up within her, she breaks and runs to mingle it with his in an embrace that only extends the game, forgiving, seeking his forgiveness, making up. Round two.

And so, encouraged by Paul's suggestion that by violating the intention of the scene they might *discover* intention, they have found emotions that surprised them, meanings that surprised them, activities to dramatize the inner life of the scene, and have experienced firsthand the terrible cost in this mother and son's dependency and the terrifying comfort it supplies.

After the apology at the bedroom door the energy flattens. Amanda and Tom return to the table like cows to their stanchions and sit down to talk for the next several pages. I notice Michael Ballhaus across the room. He is wearing the thinnest of smiles and is studying his watch again through the purple agony of a diver caught in the kelp with his air hose cut: they seem bound to stay rooted forever to that table, and rooted with them is his cinematic dream. After an eternity the scene ends. They have been sitting so long they have to do yoga stretches.

PAUL: Not uninteresting. I'm not in *love* with a five-page scene at a table, but it's not boring—it's very full. Her long trip down the hall proves that *movement* away doesn't take *tension* away. But I don't want to impose a lot of movement if it wrenches the scene for you. Smile, Michael! Think what a delicious challenge this can be—like photographing rocks.

JOHN: When it's there emotionally, it really doesn't matter where we are. Or it does. If moving doesn't lose tension, maybe I shouldn't even sit to drink my coffee.

JOANNE: In that case I wouldn't go back to my room.

PAUL: Let me just think.

JOANNE: It's getting too complicated. Too many twists and turns. I'd like to try it once where we don't move at all.

PAUL: Be my guest.

I see Michael Ballhaus turn and have a conversation with the wall, but I can't hear what he's saying. When they repeat the scene they don't even budge till the end, when Tom has to get up to leave. John discovers a way of speaking this time through that he will keep until the film is shot—the speech of reason: his voice soft, calming, unruffled, patient, polite, he tries with all his heart to explain himself, and even when she buzzes at him, he forces himself to endure it the way a leper endures flies, explaining and explaining and nearly telling the truth. Across the room Michael surfaces, streaming with kelp, and, seeing them still at the table, breathes deeply and dives again. The scene ends.

"From the top, once more," Paul says, and when they finish he requests it once again. And again, for a sixth, seventh, eighth time. I see the burden of the morning dragged toward noon. As the rehearsal goes on, disparate details of the scene catch fleeting breath, then die, wet kindling in a fire, but the scene as a whole eludes them. All at once Paul notices Karen knitting all alone near the buffet.

PAUL: Karen! My God! I'm sorry! We're not going to get to you for hours!

I'm reminded of that gentle, immaculate professional, Boris Karloff, patiently reading his *Manchester Guardian* in a rehearsal hall at CBS where he had been forgotten, and saying, upon being discovered there and asked why he hadn't gone home, "But nobody thaid I'd been dithmithed."

PAUL: I'm eating wood. I am. I'm eating wood and nobody cares!

He is, poor fellow. He's eating wood—a piece of pine he has lifted without thinking from a pile of scrap sweepings in a trash can. He has been munching it absently, like sugarcane.

JOANNE [*to Paul*]: So what did you think of the scene?

JOHN [*who thinks she means him*]: I don't know, I don't know! It feels all right at the table, at least when she's telling him things she's never told anyone.

JOANNE: That's the only truthful moment they have. I think the thing in her heart that she can't describe is the beauty she once knew.

JOHN: And I think what's in *his* heart is the truth he wants to tell her instead of "I go to the movies." He *almost* tells her what he really does, but he can't get it out. He respects her too much.

JOANNE: And when I said, "Where are you going?" and I saw your face, suddenly I thought, "Where *is* he going?" Aren't there tiny little moments where she knows?

Paul detaches himself from a pillar against which he has been leaning, like Hud.

PAUL: Yes to all of the above. But it's so difficult to find a handle on how to get into the body of it. On the one hand, it's going to be the most important talk they've ever had, not like their usual breakfast talk. She knows it. Tom feels it. He senses it's got an import of a very special kind, and it has because she's seen that letter from the Merchant Marine, and he doesn't know that yet. But on the other hand, the language is "Promise you'll never be a drunkard . . . shredded wheat . . . Eat a bowl of Purina . . . Christian adults want superior things." It's language that doesn't accommodate a slowly accumulating sense of nervous tension at all, and it jumps all over the place before it lets her get to the point.

JOANNE: So do you like it better sitting down or getting up or what?

PAUL: Irrelevant. None of that's going to make the scene work. There's just too much going on.

He flops down beside the others. The scene that took hold at the start of the day is now waterlogged and they are all feeling a funk settling in like a front of bad weather.

PAUL: I don't want to be a traffic cop.

JOANNE: Are we going to take a break now?

PAUL: No we are not going to take a break now. We are going to sit here now and keep talking, except I have nothing to say. I don't know how to help you guys. I feel impoverished.

The funk thickens and spreads like gray Jell-O through the room, locking them into a depressed tableau.

JOANNE [*nearly strangling on what she is chewing*]: Have a rice cake. They're the cure for everything.

Paul groans and gives her a lost look.

PAUL: Send a package to Reagan.

JOANNE: It's terrible. I keep thinking I'm really exploring, then all of a sudden I come up bang against the wall of my old performance, get caught in all my old intentions. I just wish I could break out. It's always been the toughest scene for me. From the beginning. So many switches! So many ins and outs! The next time we go through it, I want to go back into my bedroom. That really began to work for me, if that worked for you, John.

JOHN [*noticing Michael Ballhaus*]: Michael! When you report for rehearsal would you at least bring a viewfinder and a light meter so you look as if you're doing something?

PAUL: Michael, get over here. Get the gag out of your mouth and tell us what to do.

JOHN: Or do you even care what happens to us all!

MICHAEL: I care a lot. I am desperate. Five pages sitting at a table makes me desperate.

He barrels in among them and starts telling John how to act the scene, which amazes me. Paul's face reveals nothing.

MICHAEL: If you really wanted to tell her the truth you would have to get away from her to do it. If you wanted to say what is really in your heart instead of "I go to the movies," if you wanted to tell her, "Mother, I have this sixteen-year-old boy," you wouldn't just say it at the table.

JOHN: I think he's too scared to get up. I don't think they'd move. I don't think they'd even breathe.

MICHAEL: He has slept one hour! He's a wreck! He would get up from the table!

PAUL: Or he'd sit down. Michael, you can't just make an actor get up in a scene—and when he's up, there's an element of shitkicking about him that makes me like it better when he's down.

JOANNE: It's certainly easier to play.

MICHAEL: But everybody is talking as though this were reality. We are not talking about reality. When we started to talk about this movie we said, "It's memory, it all has to do with memory." So how would he remember a scene like this? In his memory would he be looking at himself sitting at a table? No! He would be remembering pieces of things— his mother—other things around him. What possibilities do we have to show how he remembers? Is it as though we were in a circle, and he is in the center of the circle, and Amanda is moving around him, around and around, talking, talking, talking? Or is it something else? I mean, *crazy* things like that he would remember! I am trying to think, in every scene, how we can make it even more how he remembers—

PAUL: But the character out here doing the remembering is also remembering himself.

MICHAEL: But do we have to be so logical? Can't we be freer? Can't we show how he *imagines* how he was? Must he only remember that he was sitting down? I have no solutions yet for a lot of scenes, but this goes through my mind constantly when I am watching, whenever I am reading: *"How can we with the camera create more memory?"* It kind of frees you to try anything when you feel that way because you see there are no limits. And I am wondering what you are thinking about it.

PAUL: I'm thinking my brain went cross-eyed.

Drew Rosenberg, the production assistant, comes in to take orders for lunch and reminds Paul that he has a videotaping at one o'clock with Liz Smith of NBC's *Live at Five* for delayed telecast this afternoon. Paul chortles at this reminder, glad for the break in mood and gleeful about a plot he is hatching for this interview. It will be his first public response to a scurrilous rumor that boiled from the bowels of the *New York Post,* whose owner, Rupert Murdoch, is the windmill monster in the New-man crusade for Truer Truth in Journalism.

JOHN: The *Post?* The *Post?* I wouldn't miss an issue of it! I am never without it! I have it sent to me everywhere in the world!

This very *Post,* in its sleepless quest for the news that elevates even as it informs, has wrapped itself with the determined voraciousness of a vampire bat around a glancing remark in Sunday's *New York Times* that Paul Newman is "a lean 5'-11"." Ridiculous, snorted the *Post:* "Anyone who has met Paul face to face says he has never hit 5'-11" except in heels." And to back up this scoffery, the paper has offered one thousand dollars to charity for every inch Paul stands above 5'-8", thereby darkly implying that he is, in *fact,* 5'-8", and that is a diminution that demands, if not a duel, equivalent satisfaction if honor is ever to survive.

As Paul ascends from our dungeon to his waiting car, he unrips a fearsome plot: "We're going to have a little scam here, fellas—let 'em know that real men don't eat quiche, and real men don't bet no measly thousand dollars a inch on nothin'! I'm upping the ante—let's start playing hardball! A *hundred* thousand an inch, fellas, for every inch they're wrong! Ever see a newspaper blink?" And he's gone, the funk of rehearsal lifted.

I skip lunch to write all this and to note some observations from this morning:

"Note to myself: Michael vs. Paul. The difference in two sensibilities. Michael represents the other half of the split Paul sees in himself as dramatized by Thomas Mann's *Tonio Kroeger,* a story that haunts him and mirrors his dilemma. In the story, the logical, cool, 'blue-eyed people' of northern Europe—successful, reserved, bourgeois, conventional, socially admired—stand in eternal opposition to the free, warm, artistic, 'brown-eyed people,' the dreamers and 'bohemians' of the south. Torn in two directions throughout his growing up, these sides continue to struggle in Paul even as they did in Tonio, irreconcilably but persisting in an uneasy coexistence—never satisfied, always guilty, forever accusing each other of fraudulence, allowing no peace—while at the same time harboring an unrequited, life-long, and loving 'gentle envy' of each other.

"So here is Michael, the 'Artist,' visionary of the untrammeled Joycean cinema, the brown-eyed side of Paul, and here is Paul, the traditionalist side of him ascendant now, the minimalist, the purist, caught in creative contortion because Michael is daring him to make a choice, not only in favor of freewheeling cinematic innovation, but also of the brown-eyed, creative, spontaneous, and joyful side of his own nature, of heart over brain, involvement over detachment, urging him, indeed, to take a chance on a visual experiment that carries no guarantees except the guarantee that, whatever his choice, he will not hear the inner cry of 'Fraud!' Considering this challenge, yet concerned that an audience somewhere might find offensive too bold an assault on traditional interpretations of the play, Paul hesitates to go too far, hesitates to add to the fine pure linen of what he thinks was Tennessee's intention, too much embroidery of his own. It's an important moment, not only because style, in this case, is content, but because the issue goes straight to the seismic crack in Paul, the aesthetic and personal impasse he has never been able to relieve, whose tension may be what lends to his art, side by side with the less frequent flashes of an uninhibited joy, the peculiar qualities of virtue and uprightness, warning and apartness, reticence, calculation, regret, and mistrust that so mark him.

"Another note to myself: Paul: detached on the surface but his palms still sweat, T-shirts still get changed three times in the course of any scene he acts in, but the salt line in the shoes is gone. Improvement or only a thicker cover-up? Without emotion he speaks of emotion, and people who can't get through think he is cold. He is also deeply assailable, defenseless really, and for all his independence, dependent. As a director, his words don't always show you his vision, or put you beside him at the oars. His images often lack 'juice.' He doesn't prime actors like pumps by sharing dreams, affective memories, colorful allusions. He casts words sparingly, like fishing lures, to the precise center of the pool where his trout is waiting, and offers the bare hook only, take it or leave it: a gesture, a piece of behavior—sometimes unexplained, an active verb. But to read his words is only half the story. Voice matters more. And hands. He directs by capillary action: you don't get 'it,' you get *him*. He eludes capture in quotation, imitation, anecdote. He's not Cagney or Bogart, Barrymore or Fields. How can anyone imitate dependability? Spectacular as the shell of him may be, his essence is what makes him recognizable—that disciplined 'thing,' whatever it is, that lets him ride, one foot on each, the twin chariots of his divided self."

I finish my writing and find Paul, back from his interview with Liz Smith, on the production phone in the hall. The receiver is jammed to his ear as he listens—over the screaming of saws in the woodshop—to the head of orthopedics at New York Hospital. "Gotcha!" says Paul to the doctor. "Gotcha! Gotcha!" making notes all over his script. He is grinning as he hangs up and reports to me what he just heard: "He thinks I can make it to a cool six feet if I hang upside down in gravity boots the night before I'm measured, then do it again the next morning!" It would have to be morning, according to the doctor—when spines are long and fluids that have poured through the system all night still lie in intervertebral caverns like floodwaters in fields of paddy, extending the back an extra inch or even two. Once measured, Paul will be free to shrink back down to his normal 5'-10¼", meanwhile having gleefully hustled the *Post* out of four hundred thousand dollars for charity! As I climb to the commissary for a sandwich, I look back down the hall and can almost see Rupert Murdoch's ankle in Paul's teeth. Paul is growling over it, tossing it this way and that. A gruesome sight.

When I return to Stage I, I sense something very peculiar. I see it first in the faces on the sidelines, faces of awe, like the ones I imagine at Pompeii, and in the bodies, frozen at the moment of disaster like blast silhouettes on a wall. The scene they are watching is the "Mommy, I'm Sorry" one we watched all morning, but now there's the darkness of plague at the table, and two strangers are murdering each other, shooting venom at each other's eyes like spitting cobras. My *brain* tells me it's Joanne and John, but The Lady I knew has gone, and so has Tom. They sit in a lethal silence, and when they break it, it's only to snarl across the table in a grisly *folie à deux,* clacking away like skeletons playing a game of Truth. The game seems doomed to go on forever, and the longer it does, the more their accusations mutilate. With every line they spoon themselves deeper into hell. There can be no recovery from this, no redemption, for when, at the end, John shouts his "Yes!" it's the shout of someone tearing on the rack. What started all this? I wonder. What impulse could have possibly provoked it?

"It just happened," Paul will tell me later. "I don't know which one sparked it, but it went up like a forest fire. They always take on each other's chemistry, but that first impulse was as ugly as a muddy tennis ball, and whoever slammed it back made it even uglier, and the whole scene went dark, more and more brutal. It showed me how really cruel these characters could be, and the actors weren't afraid of that, they went with it all the way: 'Oh, we fell through a trapdoor? Fine! Where's the flashlight? See that spook over there in the corner?' It demanded that kind of exploration. It was orgasmic for them, and exciting for me, and I wouldn't have shut them down for anything. But while the process was right, what they found was wrong, totally, totally wrong for this play."

PAUL: So. How do you get back to your jonquils after that one, kiddo? [*Joanne doesn't answer.*] How do you guys feel about it?

JOHN: I guess it was pretty dark, but I mean, I felt fine. I think it's a dark play. And very cruel.

PAUL: Joanne?

JOANNE: To me it's not a matter of light or dark—if Tom's dark, I'm dark too. I am simply a reflection of my children. In my life, I keep waiting for my children to tell me who I am so I can know who to be, and in the play it's the same. I don't know who Amanda is except as her children define her. I've played with three Toms now, and been three different Amandas, and it's always who my children are and who they create me to be.

Paul is silent. The tick of the freight elevator intrudes through the old wall.

PAUL: Well, I don't know who wrote that scene. What I saw was Strindberg, or Euripides, or Kafka. I kept waiting for someone to turn into a cockroach, and I sure as hell don't think that's Tennessee Williams. It was like watching a drunk hit bottom—necessary, but you don't encourage any further trips down the road. I thought it was absolutely riveting. Powerful. And it could be done that way, but it's wrong.

JOHN: Well, if what I'm doing communicates some terribly dark hatred, then it's not what I mean.

PAUL: The dark impulses are right, but you have to mute them. It's dark because of what they do, not the way they do it. I mean, when he teases her, John, he teases with respect. He watches her and he's fascinated because for all her fluttering she's arranged, by God, to hold it all together.

JOHN: Well, I think she's amazing too, and in some weird way she's funny. But see, in my family we had very funny people, but we'd never be caught laughing at them, and it didn't mean lack of respect.

PAUL: All the colors were gone, all the rainbows—

JOHN: I've seen it played that way, with rainbows. It's how they do it all the time, with a kind of light teasing.

PAUL: Well, even if that seems obvious to you, it doesn't mean they're not doing what Tennessee intended, and our oblig-ation is to improve his intention, not violate it. Isn't it funny how I invoke the playwright only when I need him in an argument, and absolutely ignore him when I don't? But he states it very clearly in your first monologue, John. "The play is memory. . . . It is sentimental, it is not realistic. In memory everything seems to happen to music. That explains the fiddle in the wings." A fiddle. What you guys gave me was a timpani magnified by a bomb-pumped X-ray laser! You also gave me an incredibly valuable exer-cise, not just for you but for me. Because it really reaf-firmed my conviction about what the tone of the film has to be: affection that somehow went astray—and the sound of a fiddle in the wings.

Fourth Day of Rehearsal

Paul comes flapping in like a flag, all in red, white, and blue, cock-a-doodle-dooing about a report in the *New York Daily News,* a newspaper he despises nearly as much as the *Post*—"Two rags in search of a toilet" is what he calls them—describing yesterday's Liz Smith interview with Paul in which he challenged the *Post* for questioning his height. "Tall Tale Time," the headline reads, and the article concludes: "When called for comment last night, the *Post* was uncharacteristically mute." Paul says, "I'll lay you sixty cents on the side that they fold like an accordion!" But our mouths, as we gorge ourselves from the buffet, are too full to say whether there are any takers. Steering John and Joanne by their elbows, and calling Mary Bailey to bring her notes, he herds them into the "dining room" and the day begins.

PAUL: John! Joanne! General notes for both of you, mostly from
   yesterday. John, we have plenty of this. [*He shakes his fist to*

demonstrate.] And plenty of this. [*He subsides in despair.*] But what we don't have, and I think they'll be gold for you, are moments when you respond to her attention, when you try to comfort *her,* enjoy her, encourage her, help her. Those will be gold for all of us. And Joanne, generally the prattle works, the bustling works, but at the moments of confrontation you can think *this.* [*He smashes out with a right hook.*] But contain it. Remember The Lady. The Lady should never be lost. The way I can tell if she's there is by what you do with your hands—wonderful things that aren't you at all, that come right out of The Lady.

Whenever Joanne thinks "The Lady," she conjures for herself three internal images, which, when combined, cause an immediate and seamless transformation. The ruling physical image is her Grandmother Woodward, who "had her hair marcelled, and her back never touched the chair. . . . She wore one of those Spencer corsets, and I can't imagine why I would ever have embraced her, except you were supposed to, but I remember embracing this *cage!* . . . When you sit in those things, you can't bend. You have to get up in one piece, and that's the way Grandmother was." The accent, and some of the spirit, arise from a second image: Maude Brink, "Aunt Dae-Dae" from Atlanta. A cordial matriarch of enormous energy and power who, at eighty-three, is still flirtatious and light-footed when the band begins to play, and is the only woman I've met whose drawl can make three vowels out of one, and sometimes four, depending on the proof of the bourbon; Paul is "Pow-ell" to her. The third image, the image of the unhealed heart, is, of course, Joanne's mother: childlike, bewildered, and tremulous with hope.

PAUL: Should we just feel our way through "Mommy, I'm Sorry," through this walking-on-eggs situation? Can we remember there's a fiddle in the wings?

They walk to their positions to start the Apology scene.

JOANNE: It's so different than it is onstage. Amanda's such a *stage* person. Oh, feel my head! Ever since my permanent there's stubble all over my head. It's all broken. I've lost half my hair!

Nevertheless, she seems much more certain today. Both actors are less inward, more awake to each other's responses, freer to move. Joanne sits like a tombstone, waiting for John's apology, and when she suddenly goes to her bedroom, Paul and the entourage follow: Mary with her script; Tony Walton, who has dropped by to discuss some scenic question and stayed; and Michael at Paul's shoulder. They surge with the scene like surf around a rock, moving in then giving way on the tide of the action. We watch Joanne build herself into a tower of regret, standing so near her we can almost hear the inner process. John comes all the way into the room this time to apologize, and we have to back up. He sits on the bench that stands in for her bed, bringing intimacy, in a shift from yesterday, bringing a golden moment for Paul. The change prompts a rush of appreciation from Joanne tender enough to let Tom tolerate her worries about his sobriety, and supportive enough to firm him up like clay into the shape she needs him to be in order to do her bidding for Laura. Subtle differences, but they bind the disconnected moments into beats.

PAUL: Wouldn't he get defensive when she says, "Promise never to become a drunkard"? I think he would because she may be right—has that occurred to you? And staying in the bedroom's nifty, Joanne. But don't even move till you get that promise out of him.

The action moves them back to the dining room.

PAUL: Now feed him! Cereal! Cream! Start the avalanche! And John, *comfort her with your willingness to hear!* Surprise her! Surprise me!

Some impulse sweeps them into Tom's bedroom for Amanda's accusations about the letter from the Merchant Marine, and the action seems natural and right. Michael smiles, glad to see them away from that table. And when John sits on his cot to put on his shoes, it reproduces the Quarrel scene in a way that connects him to the habits of his life and makes us feel at home here. Amanda follows Tom down the hall, demanding that he bring home a gentleman caller, and we all go with her.

PAUL: Joanne, the tactile thing has to be much more selective, darting in to touch and not touching.

She thinks about it a moment and then dances in and out at John to make her delicate points.

PAUL: Yes, do that but stay in one place. Guard your exits, never give him a shot at the door. Block the door! If he tries to get out he'll have to manhandle you. Let the impulse go all the way. The scarf! The lapels! Grab hold! I don't want to turn this into an ice-skating rink but keep darting, dart in and touch him on the cheek, then back up fast so he can't get around you. And keep that dance you did yesterday, that funny little sideways medieval dance.

She is all over John, staying always just out of harm's way, fussing with his scarf, patting his lapels, brushing at his hair, darting, dancing.

JOANNE: "Down at the warehouse, aren't there some nice young men?"

JOHN: "No!"

JOANNE: "There must be—some . . ."

JOHN: "Mother—"

JOANNE: "Find out one that's clean-living—doesn't drink and—ask him out for Sister!"

JOHN: "What?"

JOANNE: "For Sister! To meet! Get acquainted!"

JOHN: "Oh, my gosh!"

JOANNE: "Will you? Will you? Will you? Will you, dear?"

JOHN: "Yes!"

PAUL: Well, we got some good stuff out of that!

At one o'clock I find myself in Joanne's dressing room. She makes calls while we lunch on sunflower seeds like a couple of parrots. Then she reveals a huge hunk of Jarlsberg cheese, pathetically concealed in a napkin. She is not a very effective contrabandista. We devour the corners of it while she tries to water, with the shampoo attachment on the sink, the five little homeless plants I have brought her, but something makes the hose go berserk, drenching us both and driving us into the hall. We can't get close enough to turn it off, but we're too cowardly to just walk away, so we stand there, clutching each other like

Hansel and Gretel, till Providence sends a workman, whistling, on his way somewhere, with a wrench in his hand.

Paul rests on the couch in the rehearsal hall. His half a tuna sandwich still lies in its container on the floor beside him—he has had another make-believe lunch. His wounds are livid in the blue fluorescence, all the purple scrapes and cuts and batterings of the years. The sunburned nose under this cruel light reveals like a veteran's medal the beer campaigns of long ago, and his line from *Sweet Bird of Youth* lifts through my mind: "Time, the enemy in us all," and I see him again as he was, barely out of his twenties, drawing that white gauze curtain across the stage in the opening moments of the play, and hear the breath of the audience falter. Then, "Oh lost, and by the wind grieved, ghost, come back again," goes through my mind, simply because it's the saddest line I know. His cheekbones are sharper than they were. I've seen the blue eyes in too many weathers for them to astonish me. They're warier now. He mocks them, as a kind of deformity. His cold, or whatever it is, hangs on and on, beleaguering him even in the sleep that's meant to cure it.

John speaks to Michael in a corner, in undertones out of deference to the figure on the couch. Jim Naughton, absent since the first reading, and the outsider now for having missed the tribal forging, comes in with a questioning look, as if, in spite of the smiles and little waves he receives from around the room, he isn't sure he's come to the right place. Joanne greets him with that special hug that welcomes you home from the wars. Paul, awake, coughs, squints at the wristwatch at the far end of his arm, then rolls to his feet.

PAUL: James! I just want you to know I am completely
    unprepared and hoping that some unsolicited burp

might waft us in the right direction. I hope you have one
to spare.

They shake hands with a gosh-golly awkwardness, swaying
from foot to foot and finally hugging. Jim asks if Paul has been
watching the World Series. Paul says no, but in case Jim should
get the wrong impression, Paul reels off the names of every
Cleveland Indian on the 1938 team. Ballplayers of another time,
and telephone numbers: he can pull them out of the air like an
autistic savant. Paul has called Jim in to begin exploration of the
Gentleman Caller scene but he has arrived too early; Joanne and
John must still run through the Annunciation scene that pre-
cedes it before Paul will be ready to work with him.

Tom, discovered alone on the fire escape, observes in a monologue to the audience how ironic it seemed—in the years that he
lived here—that while the band in the Paradise Dance Hall
across the alley continued to play "The World Is Waiting for the
Sunrise" for its young habitués restlessly awaiting their adventures, even as Tom was awaiting his, the world was waiting for
bombardments of a war that would shortly absorb them all. The
memory of Amanda breaks in: she has come out to wish on the
moon. Coyly, Tom teases her with the news she has been waiting
for forever, that he has finally invited a gentleman caller to
dinner, tomorrow night. The scene plays effortlessly, lightly,
from Joanne's first entrance to the painful moment in the parlor
when, bringing her gently down from the exultation of her
expectations, Tom implores Amanda not to hold out too much
hope, to remember that Laura is crippled and seems "different"
to other people. They finish and there is nothing to say: the
scene is as natural and simple in its line as the Apology scene was

forced, and one senses, in our enjoyment, and in the delight of
the actors playing it, that it might have been a happy one to
write. Paul whispers some notes to Mary, then moves on to the
scene that follows:

It is the next night. The apartment has been readied for
celebration. The supper is cooked. The ladies are nearly ready.
Tom, on the fire escape again, remembers the gentleman
caller—a high school acquaintance named Jim O'Connor who
shot "with such velocity through his adolescence that you would
just logically expect him to arrive at nothing short of the White
House by the time he was thirty," but who now appears doomed
to remain forever at the same shoe warehouse that Tom is
preparing to escape from. Mr. O'Connor is also "that long-
delayed but always expected" someone in Laura's life, the boy
she had secretly loved at school, without Tom's knowing, and
who christened her "Blue Roses"; she has no idea that he is the
gentleman caller whose arrival is so imminent.

Paul listens to John feeling his way through the monologue
and looks increasingly disgruntled. "Playwright identification
stuff!" he growls as the monologue ends. Everyone looks at him,
surprised.

PAUL: You want character revealed through action, not through
    words that other people say. If we can't tell who the
    gentleman caller is by how he behaves, then no descrip-
    tion's going to help the playwright. I'm thinking of cut-
    ting it out.

John looks appalled, and I see Jim set down his coffee cup
over at the buffet. The two men exchange worried glances.

PAUL: I'd really like to get rid of all three monologues that come
    in the middle of the play. You only need the ones at the

beginning and the end. It's got nothing to do with the acting, John. It's just the writing.

He walks away. The idea is so radical it shocks me; I have had no warning of it. The monologues are old friends to me, flawed perhaps, as old friends are, but comforting and familiar. To lose them because they no longer serve seems almost ungrateful. John's face is indescribable. Jim looks as though he'd just heard the engines fail at thirty thousand feet. John goes after Paul, pressing urgently for further explanations, and Michael closes in from the other side. I'm nearly tempted to write down: "Paul turns at bay!"

PAUL: Well, Tennessee himself said he just stuck those monologues in to cover costume changes, and we don't have that problem on the screen. Cutting them out would give the film a symmetry—one memory that flows in a straight line from the first monologue to the last. We'd never have to interrupt the story. The "Paradise Dance Hall" one was always valid because it told you Tom was a poet, but I'd have to cut that too if I cut the others. You can't just keep one monologue sticking up in the middle of the play like a leftover iceberg. The one you just did provides some incidental information about the gentleman caller, but whether keeping three monologues for that is worth it, I don't know.

Jim turns away looking desperate. It's not only "incidental" information that this monologue contains; it's the only objective history we are given about a character we meet only once, who is never shown in a context of his own, whose function is only as a catalyst of false hope and for the shattering of the family in the failure of that hope, and who must carry the burden of initiative for as long as he's on the screen. Therefore any hint the playwright can provide about O'Connor's personality, any insight the audience can be given to supply a background, becomes a tremendous boon to the actor.

Paul promises to postpone his decision and the room relaxes a little. Rehearsal goes on. Having finished the offending monologue, John stops to speak quietly with Michael Ballhaus while Paul goes to work with Joanne and Karen on the passage that follows, in which Laura and Amanda finish dressing for the gentleman caller's arrival. I see John beckon to Jim to join him in the little anteroom off the main rehearsal hall, then shut the door. Behind it, their voices are loud enough to make it hard for Paul to concentrate. Joanne is trying to persuade him to let her "rouge" Laura's face to make her as pretty as possible for the gentleman caller—she wants to pinch her cheeks to pinken them, the way Scarlett O'Hara did, and she makes Paul pretend to be Laura so she can show Karen what she means. He puckers up and submits while Joanne pinches away, then finishes her lecture-demonstration by licking a finger and twisting a spit curl in his hair. He bolts and everyone laughs.

Now Joanne is pretending to show off her dress, an antique cotillion gown that nobody has seen yet and that won't be ready till next week. She carries a crumpled newspaper to represent a bouquet of yellow jonquils. "Accent!" Paul reminds her. "Three vowels for every one." So, blocking out the voices from the anteroom, Joanne passes into The Lady, and Amanda is there again, waltzing as she remembers jonquils, how she gathered them in the fields of Blue Mountain until the house was massed with them and there weren't vases enough to hold them all, how she held all the rest in her hands. She reaches back into the past to them, as though she were trying to fill her palms with their pollen so she can smear it over all the shabby objects of her life and gild them with its charm. She ends the speech by "seeing" again the picture of her husband on the wall, and devastates us with her final line: "Malaria fever, your father, and jonquils." Paul tells her not to move so much. She needs to move, she says; those vases in the house were everywhere. "Fine," he says, "but constrict it." He tells her to anchor her feet, so she floats in a tiny circle, revolving like the enameled figurine of a shepherdess on a gilded music box. Then Paul performs for Karen the way he wants her to dramatize her shyness, by backing up until she can "wrap the corner around her," then sliding sideways along the wall to escape when Amanda orders her to answer the bell and let the gentleman caller in.

It's time for Jim's entrance. Paul goes to the anteroom, where the fire of the crisis still crackles, and calls out, "Rise and shine!" John and Jim stop talking and, after a moment, open the door. He doesn't ask them what they've been saying, doesn't admit he's even heard them; he just goes to lean on a pillar, arms akimbo, falling into Hud again as they come by to start their scene. I wonder how they can all go on while the problem of the monologues stays unresolved.

I find myself wishing he'd ask my opinion, and my thoughts begin to drift into the past. I remember how, on any set I visited where he was working, he'd wander over and ask, "What do you think?" Or he'd pull me into his dressing-room trailer with an I-won't-take-no-for-an-answer hand and ask me to write for him, in secret, some new line of dialogue "that a human mouth can at least get its lips around" and take the credit himself so I wouldn't "get in trouble with the Guild." Or he'd drag me to the previews of his pictures in palmy little towns with one streetlight, our T-shirts stretched over freezing cans of smuggled beer, and, "What do you think?" he'd ask.

All I want to do is sleep. I don't want to see him as a man who has become the work he does. I want to remember the fun we had when they still lived in walk-ups and made their own bookshelves and taught me to swallow spoonfuls of Vicks VapoRub for colds, and the sound those beer cans made rolling down the theatre aisles in the middle of those previews. Then, even as I'm thinking how sad it is that such things seldom happen anymore, he comes moping across the floor to me and asks, "What do you think?" The answer doesn't matter; I think I tell him I like the monologues, and I tell him why. And I think he tells me I'm wrong. In the end he'll decide to keep them, and credit Henry Mancini for helping to make it possible: "His music telegraphed the transitions to the past in such an arresting way, they added to the whole flow of the picture."

Nothing's happening in the room. Paul has left my side and gone to the buffet to peel an orange. Joanne notices the lull. "Hey, Paul!" she cries. "What are we doing, or are you just going to eat?" He's thinking, he says, and it's easier with an orange in his mouth. The Gentleman Caller scene is finally upon him, a scene that suspends the primary conflict of the play and can stop the play entirely if the actors fail to fascinate. The responsibility placed on the one playing Jim O'Connor is enormous, and the temptation to overact or sentimentalize in order to make the scene appear more active than it is has often made it seem to be less about hope lifted and hope lost and more about the eternity that Tom and Amanda are missing from the stage. Mary Bailey reminds Paul of the time. He has to fly down to Atlanta for this weekend's Trans-Am race, so decides to quit while he's ahead, and rehearsal ends.

Joanne hates to fly, so she has invited me to accompany her on the overnight train. I have assembled, from food purveyors all over the city, a gargantuan picnic for our journey: chicken, champagne, and a tarte Tatin large enough for eight. Our trip is wonderful: train smells, the smells of childhood, and the wonder of berths that pull down and of sinks that disappear into the wall. We talk, we toast each other, we listen to the rattling quiet, two heads swaying over two swaying books.

It rains monotonously most of the weekend, a gentle damp that doesn't so much fall as break out on our skins like sweat. Aunt Dae-Dae appears at the track. She arrives in the limousine Joanne has hired and plunges through the barriers set up to keep back the fans, to hug her "Pow-ell" in his trailer while he's still suiting up for his race. Then she seizes my umbrella arm with one jeweled hand and hauls Joanne along with the other, and marches us proudly along over muddy ruts and under streaming groves from one hospitality tent to another, whether we're invited or not, to compare the canapés and sample the chilis, and by the last cloudburst, people she hadn't known ten minutes earlier all have her address folded into their pockets. Joanne smiles at me over her head, as if to say, "You see? The Lady!"

Paul has a miserable time. As soon as his race is called the skies open to let down the final honest downpour of the day and he comes off the track on the pace lap, before the race even starts. When we reach him, soaked and begrimed and disgusted, he says: "My goddam oil radiator's in a sleeve on the side of my door. Car gets anywhere near speed, it sucks so much rain onto that hot pipe there's steam all over the windshield. I couldn't even tell where I was. All I could do was stay out of the way and try to get back to the pits." End of adventure.

A depressing ride back to the motel. Not being needed for the Gentleman Caller scene, Joanne will return to New York alone on the train and I will fly back with Paul. He kisses her goodbye as she leaves to have supper with Dae-Dae, then goes to pack. We're late getting to the airport, and we have to run for the plane. I can see that the pain in his ribs is back from all the test-driving he did, but he won't give up his suitcase until I yank it out of his hand. Just before we reach the gate he does a squealie into a newsstand and asks me to buy him *Newsweek*.

He's embarrassed to buy it himself because there's an article in it about him: a long interview by David Ansen and his review of *The Color of Money.*

Once on board, he waits till the lights have gone out and the movie has begun before he opens the magazine. He sits next to me turning the pages, the only passenger in our row whose reading light is on. He has covered the picture of Paul Newman with his hand so no one can tell what he's reading.

Fifth
Day of
Rehearsal

When I come in I see that Paul, who's had to take his concentration south a thousand miles for three days in a muddy trailer at the side of a rainy track, looks as if he's never been away.

PAUL: Karen! Jim! Let's put these two chairs facing each other to get some idea of the distance between you. It's all about narrowing distances, then presenting her with the abyss.

He picks up the chairs and carries them himself. Michael Ballhaus, with his sweet smile, comes over to help. He reminds Paul that the only light source will be the candelabrum on the floor so he mustn't place the actors too far apart.

PAUL: But wouldn't it be interesting if you only heard voices and hardly saw them at all at the beginning? Then gradually they edge closer. First you see Jim, then after a long time, Karen.

JIM: Why don't we work with candles now and really see where
we are?

PAUL: Nifty notion.

Magically, candles appear. Mary turns off the blue fluorescence overhead and in the darkness Paul lights a candle, then
another. It's like a ceremony that brings on its own silence, and
as the glow begins to spread, faces soften, and Paul draws back
from the lighted circle. I can barely make out Jim at the edge of
it, and Karen is just a darker patch on the darkness. Jim clears
his throat, drums his fingers, sends a crinkled smile to where
she is across the candle flames, and says his first line. Michael's
shoes edge in beside Paul's.

MICHAEL [*sotto voce*]: This is really wonderful. We had in the
dining room five pages with two people sitting at a table.
Now we are going to have nine pages with two other
people sitting on the floor. Thank God for variety.

Paul lets them fumble their way through the scene once
without interrupting. Then he sits down with them to give
notes.

PAUL: I'd like to get the sense that their behavior's just a mask to
cover their flaws. His openness and bigness is his deception, Jim, his defense against discovery, just as staying out
of the candlelight is hers. They brush together, brush
again, and each time they leave a little more of their
humanity on each other. They're like two flowers, closed at
the beginning, that open up petal by petal, then snap shut
at the end because they have come too far. Now, having
said that, let's try to muddy it up.

In brief, the events are these: while Laura knows now that the gentleman caller is the boy she had loved at school, he hasn't recognized her yet. After an abortive supper during which Laura, overcome by emotion, has fled to the parlor, Amanda, who has transformed herself into a travesty of girlish southern charm, sends the gentleman caller to find Laura and to take her some dandelion wine to help her recover. Laura ventures into the candlelight only reluctantly, then shyly confides that she is the girl he called Blue Roses once when she had pleurosis, the one whose leg brace made such an awful clump when she limped into singing class late. Vaingloriously, talking mainly to himself, the gentleman caller encourages her to overcome her inferiority complex, as he claims to have overcome his, and to admit how special she is. They reminisce. He sings. As she opens up to him, her sweetness releases his own and he becomes more real. He is moved to waltz with her, but in dancing past the table where he has set it down, he breaks the little glass unicorn she has given him to hold. He kisses her, not knowing she has never been kissed before. Her response frightens him, as does his own response to her. He tells her he is engaged and can never see her again. She gives him the broken unicorn and he leaves. And so a connection that might have held answers for them both is severed before it begins, and with it, all Amanda's dreams for Laura's happiness dissolve.

PAUL: So, Jim, listen to yourself at the beginning. Show her how smart you are. Don't be interested in her at all. And Karen, when he starts talking about your shyness and you ask if he's kept up with his singing, it's to *stop* him. Don't make it an invitation—put roadblocks in the way! All through the scene, fight the connection.

JIM: Great! He's all wrapped up in himself! "You got a problem?

I'll solve it!" I think he plays with her the way he plays with Tom. Tom's hopeless, so he loves to play with him and call him Shakespeare.

PAUL: Karen, why did you get up at the beginning of the scene?

KAREN: I wanted to get away from him. I wanted to run to the fire escape.

PAUL: If you want to escape, run—but run in one place. Maybe a tiny move backward off the floor and onto the hassock— that's running for Laura. But never show him your limp till you're sure he isn't seeing it anymore. Maybe you can even be on your feet when he finds you—Jim, misinterpret the fact that she's up as a sign that she's feeling better. Karen, come see the model of the set so you can find your hiding places.

We all blink at the brightness when Mary Bailey turns on the fluorescence again so Karen can study the model and fix her mind on how her "home" will look. While she lingers there with Paul, Jim breaks away to prowl, studying the buffet, the sink, the old refrigerator. He tosses his coffee cup into the air and catches it again, tosses and catches it, looping it sometimes behind his back and catching it over a shoulder, working off energy, showing off his skill. I think he must still be coping with some feeling of estrangement, hoping for someone to reach out and draw him closer to the hearth.

They start the scene from the top. Hearing Jim "enter," Karen scrabbles across the floor to hide where a curtain will hang. Jim brings in the lighted candelabrum and the glass of dandelion wine.

JIM: Where do you want me to put these candles down?

PAUL: Hold them up like a beacon till you see her, then take a step toward her and offer her the wine.

Paul calls for Michael, who appears like Mephisto out of the dark. Paul wonders if it would seem too artificial to exaggerate the threat to Laura by certain movements of the camera.

PAUL: If he takes just one step toward the lens, and at the same time we shove the camera in on him three feet, it'll look as if he's really attacking, which is how it feels to her; and if we pull away from her three feet, just as she's taking one step back, it'll look as if she's backing away from a fire, and that's how it feels to him. That's nearly how they see each other here.

Michael appears enthused and a little surprised at this sudden visual initiative from the "other side" of Paul.

JIM: Will it work?

PAUL: We'll know when we see it. Back off now, Jim. If she won't take the wine from your hand, put it down—just let her come and take it, let her do the edging toward you. Okay, let's sit down.

They sit on cushions several yards apart.

PAUL: Jim, in these first few beats your intention is "Sing for your supper, pay for your meal." And Karen, just watch— watch him, watch your flight distance, make sure you can get away.

I have seldom seen actors listen the way these do, or watch with such undefended eyes. I have no idea how, after the years

they have spent on this play, they have managed to stay so open
to new suggestions. Karen, for all her professionalism and skill,
is pure, intuitive responsiveness; and Jim, while a little more
watchful, is, for all his experience and his top-banana, off-to-
Buffalo veneer, as receptive to Paul as a virgin.

PAUL: Let's go on. Just sitting where we are.

They *have* been going on—in the silence of the pause—
Karen secretly watching this unfamiliar creature, Jim noisily
shifting his body around in a futile quest for a comfortable
position and finally lacing his hands behind his head and lying, with a sigh, "I'm comfortable as a cow." Paul laughs in appreciation. Jim asks if he can sit on a chair, but Paul won't
let him.

JIM: I hate the floor. My body wasn't *made* to sit on a floor. Lie on
     it, yes. Lounge against a chair, okay. But not *sit on the floor!*
     At Williamstown I sat with these big lumpy shoes crossed
     in front of me and they pitched me back so far I thought I'd
     fall on my head.

Just talk—trying to let Paul know him better, or so I guess.
Michael wants him on the floor too, so he can bind him to Karen
in a circular dolly shot, which, as the camera comes closer, will
gradually reduce the visual distance between them as revelations
are unveiled, finally winding Laura and the gentleman caller, by
means of the camera alone, into a tight web of intimacy. Paul has
worries about "holding actors hostage to the camera" and favors
a "looser" solution.

They advance into the scene. Jim takes a pack of Wrigley's
gum from his pocket and, after thinking it over a moment,

thrusts a stick of it at Laura: "Say, would you care for a piece of chewing gum?"

PAUL: Do it for yourself. Don't share it.

JIM: When do I ask if she wants some?

PAUL: Have it practically in your mouth before you think of it, then offer it to her as an afterthought.

JIM [*laughing*]: Boy, he doesn't ask permission to do anything, does he?

He tries and his timing is hilarious.

PAUL [*laughing*]: You know what he is? He's not heterosexual, or homosexual, he's *solo*sexual! I heard this guy on television once who said, "I'm solosexual and I'm glad—because I know every time I go home, I'm going to score!" [*Everyone laughs.*] Get off on yourself, Jim! Whatever you do, it's for you—even when you stomp around the room being *big,* entertaining her with your theories about her inferiority complex, it's all for you.

JIM: Well, I think this guy takes it very seriously, so I don't know what you mean when you say "entertain her."

PAUL: Well, a singer takes his singing very seriously too, but he sings to entertain people. I mean in that sense. So sing an aria about her inferiority complex. I'd like to see that he thinks he's the one who's fixing her, who's building up her willingness to experiment.

KAREN: It's funny how safe I feel whenever he's too involved with himself to notice me. When he's not, that's when I really have to watch him.

PAUL: Jim! Be more involved in the chewing-gum paper. Fold it. Refold it. Torture it. It'll help you postpone any contact. When you finally give her the gum, do it like a dog bringing a slipper in its teeth. Do it like Groucho—don't get off your knees.

They hack their way through to the end of the scene; it's a forced march, full of effort, long and dull in places, but there are little flares of summer lightning to show that the sky is charged and illuminate discoveries along the way. When they finish, Paul rallies them again:

PAUL: Let's talk. If each beat takes the same time, the same weight, the same consideration, they all lose force and the whole scene goes astray. Karen, does it ever occur to Laura that the glass menagerie isn't an answer? While she's telling him how wonderful it is to fill up her life with those little glass animals, find the specific moment when she knows it isn't working for her at all, and let us see it. And also, Jim, it's the way she talks about it that lets you know you want to be close to her.

JIM: When Laura's talking about the horse—

KAREN: That's the first time the flowers really open—

PAUL: Yours too, Jim. Full bloom.

JIM: The only thing that's troubling me is that I don't want it to look as if I'm throwing the make on her.

PAUL: In a way, you are: she's suddenly a leading lady—his expectations *have* to turn sexual! He's not really hearing her—he's dancing with her in his head while she's still talking about unicorns—so dance with her before you dance with her. And Karen, the thing that really happens in this scene for you is just that you finally become—willing. Willing to be willing.

They dance and the scene becomes sexual. Jim allows himself to be stirred by her, and Karen, with Laura's dead defeated eyes coming alive at last to his kindness, begins to be willing; and the more willing she is, the more healthy she seems to become until I see the possibility for resurrection. If we can believe in that completely, then the "closing of the flowers" when the gentleman caller leaves will seem like her ultimate entombment, and if that can happen, the film could achieve tragedy.

Lunch break. John Malkovich comes in with his face shorn of his mustache, his beard, and many of his years, just white, white skin and youth.

PAUL: My God!

JOHN: Oh, you haven't seen it.

Tony Walton enters hard on John's heels, bringing samples of a variety of glass unicorns. Since the action calls for the unicorn's horn to be broken, Paul selects the one that will look best without one, and Tony, considering the breakage anticipated when a new unicorn will be required for every shot, asks Paul how many to order.

PAUL: Get a dozen. Eighteen. Two dozen. How much are they?

TONY: We got a very good deal.

PAUL: Get ninety-six.

Someone else presents him, for his approval, a photograph in an antique oval frame of John as the father who "fell in love with long distance."

PAUL: Who shot this?

MICHAEL: I did.

PAUL: I like the highlight being the hat, but I'd like the face a little more masked, a little more hidden. I'd like him in a seersucker jacket with a yellow bow tie.

MICHAEL [*talking Paul into the corner*]: Can I tell you I am still a little concerned, even though it's getting better, that if Jim and Karen will be sitting for more than twenty minutes talking—

He keeps after Paul with the same chronic lament, like a patient in an emergency room shyly plucking at a busy intern's sleeve to get him to look at the fishhook in his throat.

MICHAEL: —I will be able to give you only wonderful actors giving a wonderful performance, but nothing very wonderful with the camera.

PAUL: And maybe that's all we were ever meant to have, Michael.

The rejoinder worries me: is he presenting the bottom line, preparing to preside at the death of Michael's ambitions? Or is he simply restating the ambitions he began with, with the resignation of a man who knows his limits? He breaks away from the crowd congealing around him and goes to the buffet to pour a cup of tea. Seeing him alone for a moment, I sidle over to take my slice of him.

STEWART: That scene takes an eternity!

PAUL: I saw your eyes close. Twice.

STEWART: Me? My eyes didn't close. Oh, sometimes when I listen I *hear* better with them closed. It just seems pale next to all the other scenes. It's in the writing: no volatility, and it seems to take forever to make its point. It always has, no matter who's played it, at least to me.

PAUL: Don't be deceived. What's happening is subtle, but it's happening. Just wait. Each time Karen goes through it she releases something else—so small—so sure—just little tiny signals, from the telegraph poles we talked about, of her future disintegration—but seen in miniature. Watch her hands, the fluttery little things around her mouth. Watch her limp, which I thought would not be reducible: it'll take her a couple of weeks to unhook that leg entirely and take the splint out of her knee, but every time it's subtler. Her way of working is fascinating—nearly imperceptible but with little flickers of growth—and I don't want to tamper with the mechanism. I don't want to hurry it—

I expect him to add: "Just to keep you awake," but he doesn't. I ask about Jim.

PAUL: I sense very much that he wants to be directed but I'm not sure how to go about it because I don't want to tamper with him either. There's so much of his own personality in this character that he doesn't have to crawl very far out of his skin to create physicalizations for himself. I don't want to give him a lot of Freudian background when he's giving me precisely what I want.

STEWART: He just comes complete with the equipment?

PAUL: I don't know how to help him become any more himself when he's already there. The trip is from New York to Los Angeles and the guy's already in Chicago the second he walks in the room.

STEWART: But you say you think he wants to be directed. How are you going to direct him?

PAUL: For one thing, by not telling him what I've been telling you. He'd get so self-conscious trying to be *him* that he'd never be able to do anything. He lives inside himself, so he can't see what I see from out here. Nothing I say is going to seem like enough for him. All I can do is give him little behavioral things, little beats inside of scenes—just to let him know I'm paying attention. When you were out of the room before, I asked him to examine the crease in his pants, and what he did was so right for that character that I laughed! He almost can't do anything wrong, and he comes up with marvelous things: when he said before, "I don't know when to take off my coat because if I do it too early, it'll look as though I want a little action," I didn't help. I just let him alone. And you saw, while he was standing there telling her about his disappointments, he got so involved that he started to take off the coat, got it halfway over his shoulders, then just left it there, wrapped around his arms like a straitjacket, till he got through. Now that seems insignificant, but all those choices, whether they're conscious or not, add up to that character, and when I see people working like that, I just let them alone. Let them find their own comfort in what they're doing and know it's all going to be just fine. I simply have to be patient, appreciate them for working in the big arena, and let them move at their own pace in the center ring. Meanwhile, it wouldn't hurt you to have some coffee.

STEWART: Decaf, please.

PAUL: Coffee.

While he fills my Styrofoam cup, I think how marvelous the creative process is, the conscious mind subtly inducing the unconscious to reveal itself, and the unconscious responding: that Jim's body, informed by his mind's knowledge of the character, should trap him in a jacket without instruction from him or anyone and create, with a gesture, a perfect image of the straitjacket life he can't escape from seems miraculous to me.

Joanne, back from Atlanta, comes in wearing a full khaki skirt and carrying the morning's *New York Times.* Even her complexion looks khaki, as though her whole system had been poisoned by the military. There is something about the set of her jaw that warns me to steer clear, so I go into a corner with Malkovich and make a show of cuing him on his lines instead of facing her and welcoming her home. The trouble, it seems, is the president and the announcement that, after raising at Reykjavik our hopes for world disarmament, the White House is dashing them again because Reagan wants to play Star Wars. The impracticability of it, the foolishness of it, makes us all fools too, and Joanne has taken the danger into her system like a python trying to digest a log. Her eyes have turned tawny and avoid any contact. Her voice is flat and disinterested. I wish she would scream, but I can sense that her heart holds all the threatened cities of the world and, because she is mourning them, she could only weep.

Paul calls for a run-through from the top of the script, but by the time they reach the Deception scene, Joanne's fury is racing through every artery of the play and so engorges her confrontation with Karen that I want to flee, with Laura, from what she calls "that look!" It's terrifying because it has nothing to do with the play: it's Joanne's usual response in life to personal betrayal, a form of human behavior she can neither tolerate nor understand, but there have been few other times in our association when I have seen reactions like this so disorder her art. Usually her southern breeding alone makes her eschew it, but her subtext today seems to be: "What the hell am I doing playing around here, pretending to be Amanda, when the real Ronald Reagan is likely to trash the world?" After her telephone speech at the start of the Quarrel scene Paul goes to her.

PAUL: Do you want to take a break?

JOANNE: No.

PAUL: Well, Washington may be a disaster, but two days of Aunt Dae-Dae are impressive to me. You're getting seven syllables for every one.

She groans and walks away, kicking his kneeling chair ahead of her to the exact middle of the room, where she sits down on it and establishes a zone nobody dares to enter. Paul walks right in. He respects her enough not to be intimidated, while at the same time allowing her to heal privately whatever it's possible to heal. He knows he can serve her best by persisting in his professional demands no matter what she's feeling, as though this were an ordinary day. He bends down and whispers to her. She sits very straight, paying attention. He tells her, without commenting on the source it comes from, that the anger is wonderful but to "sit on it more" at the outset, build with it less visibly so the scene doesn't get too dark. She makes no reply.

PAUL: Where is your corset?

JOANNE: What?

PAUL: To help The Lady. I thought you wanted a corset—for her posture.

JOANNE: I haven't found the right kind yet.

They start the Quarrel scene. Amanda is picking at Tom to sit up straight when suddenly John yells, "AAAGH!" and shoots out of his chair with the velocity of a body dropping through a gallows trap, and just as much at the end of his rope. It is so unexpected and funny that Paul has to blow him a kiss. "Where are you *going?*" Amanda shouts, really wanting an answer from Reagan. "Out! Out! Out!" John shouts back as he bounces from foot to foot, shoveling his "Outs!" straight at her. Later he bursts out crying in the middle of the tantrum he cannot control, completely uncorked, shouting senseless things about opium dens, mocking her with that string of fictitious cathouses, cutting at the air with the knife-edge of his hand as if he were hacking to pieces some enormous hero sandwich, and I see in his performance all that he once described but has never shown till now. It is spectacular. He roars his exit line at Joanne, hurls his coat at where the glass menagerie will be, and, in spite of the fact that he knows Paul hates this way to end the scene, drops to his knees in contrition before the damage he has done and bows his head at his own insufferable selfishness. A tableau for a curtain if I ever saw one, and bound to bring the balcony to its feet. It certainly brings me to mine. Joanne's face looks utterly uninhabited as she watches him, "underwhelmed" as they say in the Industry, and so does Paul's.

PAUL: It's just a big effect.

JOHN: He hasn't time to *think* of an effect! He can't stand himself! It's the thing I always find missing in Tom—his incredible self-disgust. I don't know what you thought of it, Joanne.

JOANNE [*dryly*]: You're right when you say it's not usually played that way. All I can do is be afraid of him.

JOHN: But maybe what you're afraid of is his madness, how really crazy he is—not the fear that he'll attack you. It's like when you catch a child doing something really, really wrong, he'll do a lot worse things instead of admitting it. It's much more his shame than his anger at her—

PAUL: Then that's what you need to show us. We don't need to understand it all, but we do need a glimpse.

JOHN: I think you'll have one.

PAUL: The scene has no sense of conclusion.

JOANNE: Isn't the conclusion that he leaves? I don't know, do you ever plan to *leave*?

JOHN: It depends on where I am with the emotion.

JOANNE: Because I think Amanda considers that performance sheer indulgence. I'd walk right out of the room when I'd had enough of it, and the impulse is to do it much sooner.

PAUL: Do it. Walk out of the room.

It doesn't take much to make her, and once gone there's no hint that she'll ever return. She sits at the far end of the rehearsal hall with her back to us, a lonely figure on a metal chair, neck bent away from the gray curls, away from us, vulnerable, trying to find some center in herself that can remove her from this day. Her cold coffee rests on the Reykjavik headline under my hand. We all resist the impulse to rush to her. Paul and John look at each other.

PAUL: Okay. I never liked it, but we'll keep the smashing of the glass menagerie because it will let me use Joanne's walk.

John, still on his knees and silent, lowers his head with relief and nods to himself several times.

Paul will tell me months later: "It was only when I saw her take that walk that I knew the scene had an ending and that he could break that glass—a true, honest, sad, funny ending. So the private thing that was happening, that anger that worked against us all that day, turned around and began to work *for* us. What Joanne brought in from somewhere outside that scene was finally the electricity that lit it."

He walks to where she is sitting and holds her hand, then asks Mary Bailey what's next. The Drunk scene. Karen puts her knitting aside and John rises to take his position. He and Joanne pass each other without a word or a glance. She glares straight ahead, walking with arms crossed tightly across her breast, and sits in a corner out of the way. Paul goes to her again and, by making a comment that has nothing to do with the work they have done today, tries to open up the maze in which she has trapped herself.

PAUL: I finally know the difference between your first phone call and the second. The first, you enjoy. The second, you're just selling.

She knows that, she says, as if it were too obvious for comment, and Paul turns his attention to the Drunk scene. He
watches it without interruption, declines to give notes at the
end, and runs the Apology scene. "In and out," he says to Joanne
when it's over, but she knows that too and walks away to brood
in a chair, staring off into space like a character in *The Sea Gull*.
He follows, stands in front of her, waiting. "It was all over the
place," she volunteers. "It was a muddle of intentions." Would
there be any profit in running it again? he wonders. But she
laughs without mirth and shakes her head no, then, slapping
her knees, says, "Let's do it!" As she rises he tries to make some
point about the scene, and the quick, blue sensitivity of his face
keeps tilting ceilingward in hope of answers as he struggles to
express himself; when he shakes his fingers for emphasis, it
looks as if he were flipping water off their tips. They repeat the
Apology scene, from the silent drinking of coffee to Tom's
strangled "Yes!" at the end, and the result doesn't add to her joy.
But Paul dances about like a juggler, keeping things airborne,
keeping things light:

PAUL: Wonderful! It's neat, Joanne! We're getting a drop on it
now! [*He walks her to her chair.*] It may not be a touchdown
yet, but at least it's a field goal, so screw you and the horse
you rode in on!

People eating celery on the other side of the room make the
dungeon resound like a stable full of clydesdales that have just
been issued their oats. Joanne turns a slow-motion gaze on
them, withering enough to make a lemon pucker up, like a
teacher I had once, Miss Purinton, whose gaze could freeze
things in midflight: there must be jacks and ping-pong balls
and mumbledy-peg knives all over New York still waiting for
permission to come down. John leaves to eat his celery outside.

Paul, Ben Franklin glasses perched on his nose, stands in for
him to show Joanne how to push Tom to the dining room table
after his apology at her bedroom door. He leans back, his full
weight filling her hands, and says, "Push me, push me, jack me
up, make me walk!" And she straight-arms him across the floor
like an overloaded wagon. John comes back and shows he's
disarmed of his celery. Paul has a word with Michael Ballhaus.
Joanne, swung around to the back of her chair, begins to let go
of her apocalypse. John wire-walks the outlines of the fire
escape, whispering a monologue to himself. Karen, on the blue
couch, knits, and Mary Bailey, deep in meditation, floats like a
snowflake just above the floor, her eyes rolled to the pipes above,
carrying the clipboard with Paul's notes close within closed
arms. They run the Annunciation scene and John's teasing of
Amanda is very funny. Paul gives comments:

PAUL: I have a note here that says, "This scene is about sweetness,
    consideration, expectancy—with 'expectancy' underlined
    three times." And it's getting there, John. Joanne, after he
    upsets you about Laura being "peculiar" go right to the
    kitchen window and pull Karen with you. Force her to wish
    on the moon. Make expectation overcome despair. John.
    Don't get bored. He is whatever he is, but he's never bored.
    You can play "Do I have to go through this again?" but be
    active about it! Joanne, you're not supposed to know how
    long this scene continues, so if he runs out of lemonade, get
    him some more—you can holler back and forth from room
    to room.

JOANNE: What time is it? Are we ever going home?

PAUL: That's a wrap. We'll pick this scene up tomorrow. My
    God! I am finally going blind. When I used to put on my
    glasses, people up close would be blurred. Now I see every

pore and follicle of you, Michael. You look like an award-winning documentary.

MICHAEL: I need to talk to you.

His smile trembles as he says it, as if to defuse his request of its urgency. He has been patient beyond patience, but all of Paul's well-meant promises of "We'll talk at lunch," "We'll take a walk on the set," have been pushed aside to take care of the free-for-all demands of other people with stronger voices.

PAUL: Can we do it tomorrow, first thing?

But Michael insists on a time. Paul promises: eight o'clock, before the actors arrive. We are driven back to town in a Teamster limousine. I sit in front, wishing I had eyes in the back of my head, like Miss Purinton, trapped in a silence that seems to go on without end. Then, gradually, I begin to hear the sound I've been hoping for, the reassuring click of knitting needles. I look out and imagine the banners of Joanne's apocalypse hanging like tattered rags on the Fifty-ninth Street Bridge. As the car sighs to an expensive halt, and its fine doors open with a hush that makes me think I've lost my hearing, Joanne asks in her crispest tone, "Is it Amanda or is it me? It's me, isn't it? What is it about me, or about me in this role, that gives me so much trouble with my Toms?" She doesn't wait for an answer. She sweeps into the lobby with a stride I haven't seen since Katharine Cornell's, and which makes me guess she'll ride upstairs alone. Somehow she knows that Paul will want to linger and make his own ascent later on. He remains in the car, or nearly, one foot on the curb and his hand on the open door.

PAUL: Joanne's never had anyone with the kind of spontaneity she
      could really bounce off of till she got Malkovich. But I

guess nothing's free. The volatility, the sudden departures and bewildering, funny shifts trip off inventions that are brilliant beyond the normal mind to comprehend, but also breed great danger for the person acting with him. You can't really hold on to him. You try to set a course and it's like spiderwebs.

He thinks of himself as a stage actor, he feels better working on the stage, but someone must have told him that in film all your inventiveness rests in what you discover mainly at the instant of performance. It's my contention that he's better than that—that he can, in fact, set his best discoveries in rehearsal, as I'm sure he does onstage, and not constantly need to avoid repetition by constantly needing to explore. I think he feels some sort of magic loss if he plays something fully in rehearsal, or repeats it, or even lets you know what he's planning to do: it's as though he had to save it for something. There are movie directors like that: "I don't want to rehearse! I want the actor to be in the moment! Film is a medium of accident!" What the hell do they think the craft of acting is?

STEWART: Maybe fear that they can't reach the moment makes them postpone confronting it. But if that's true, how can they ever know they'll be able to do it when the time comes to perform?

PAUL: That's my point. Actors like Joanne and Karen aren't afraid to commit from the beginning and keep the best of what they find as they rehearse, repeat it, freshen it, and— every time—make it seem as if it had never happened before. John's not of that school, in his film work. It doesn't make him a bad person, it just makes it risky for him and I think he shortchanges himself. But, hey, that's the way he works, and to tamper with it might get you some short-term benefits, but I think in the long run you'd lose immensely. You're better off letting him be comfortable doing it his way than impose something on him he really resists, because then he won't be able to do anything—either comfortably or right.

STEWART: So you're simply flying on faith. Interesting for somebody whose middle name has never exactly been Trust.

PAUL: Oh, everybody thinks I'm very trusting, but what they don't understand is that if I once see a section of a scene done right, even if the next rehearsals are dead on their ass and the actor never shows it to me again, it doesn't matter—once I've seen it I know it's accessible, I know it'll always be there. With John, all those little fragments have appeared—not in any totality, but enough to tell me what he's going to do in terms of Tom's struggle, his adolescent rage, his tantrums. I should probably press him to do it fully once, exactly the way he wants to do it on film, not because I need it, or Michael needs it, but because John does, just to give himself the assurance that he can do it, and not have to still be wondering when the day of shooting rolls around.

But a person of John's free spirit presents other challenges to a film director. Changing so constantly, improvising all his moves can be easily accommodated on the stage. There's nothing you have to match: fall into the orchestra pit at the matinee, you don't have to fall in again that night. But in the movies, if you fall in during a great master shot, you better fall in again in every other angle or you'll never be able to cut the film together. So the technical parameters in pictures have to be a part of the actor's process.

STEWART: John seems to believe that the actor tells the story and if the camera wants to record it, it better find him.

PAUL: Well, I'm not sure, but that can end in an actor's nightmare when he discovers that he did his best work with his back to the camera and the only one who saw it was one electrician up on a catwalk who's applauding very slowly. It's the camera that tells the story. The camera can't be denied.

STEWART: What was your first meeting like with John?

PAUL: Well, I was in the middle of *The Color of Money,* filming on location in Chicago. One Sunday morning I got on an airplane and flew down to Miami to see if he was interested enough to set time aside eight months later for a picture he'd be paid no money to do. I was bushed, and I knew I'd have to get right back on a plane again, so we only had two hours to get acquainted. He wanted to know my plan, what my approach would be, and we got in a big discussion about what makes good film directing. We finally had to chop it off. I said, "John, you know what a good film director is? He's a very tired actor who gets on a plane in Chicago and flies to Miami to get to know another actor, then flies back to Chicago and goes to work the next day. That's a good film director."

STEWART: What was his response?

PAUL: He's here, isn't he?

Paul sets his other foot down on the curb, unwinds himself from the limousine with a monosyllabic "G'night," and evaporates. A year from now he'll be telling me, "You know, Malkovich is funny. He doesn't make himself easily available, but whenever he's in New York he calls: 'Hey, you guys in town?' He and Joanne have a great simpatico. They really like each other."

I decide to walk. A mist muffles everything, halos the street-lights, makes Fifth Avenue look the way it must have in the 1880s. I pass beneath gaslights, dodge sleighs jingling by in the snow, and have dreamed my way nearly to the Plaza before I discover where I am. I listen to my heels on the pavement as I turn east, remembering a line from a play of Maxwell Anderson's that I saw here in my youth in the year I went to war, a play called *The Eve of St. Mark:*

> *Taps! Heel taps.*
> *And thus the evening ends.*

Sixth
Day of
Rehearsal

Paul and Michael Ballhaus, who have staggered in from opposite ends of the city to keep this rendezvous, are telling jokes
and drinking coffee to wake each other up when I come in. The
look they give me tells me I'm not invited. I sit down far enough
away to appear to be out of hearing and busy myself with a bagel
from yesterday's buffet. I might as well have bitten into a
grenade.

Michael is armed with a list of specifics for Paul, but a
question about Malkovich has arisen before I got here and
Michael is saying, "Don't worry about him. He will play around
and play around until the camera is on, and then he will do
anything you want." But talk of John reminds him of a problem:
he wants to know why Paul ever decided that Tom should have
his own bedroom when his cry in the play is, "I have no thing—
no single thing in my life here that I can call my *own!*" and

when, in his memoirs, Tennessee made it so plain that it was his sister Rose, not he, who had the bedroom: a very important distinction, says Michael, "because it was only there, in his sister's room, where he could go away to be by himself, away from everybody."

PAUL: What do you suggest? Do I pull down the set? A change like that would mean I'd have to reblock half the picture.

But the issue beneath the issue is Michael's continuing frustration about the imprisoning of his camera by actors in static scenes who refuse to move without strong motivation, and most of all, about the unresolved questions regarding the treatment of memory. In a scant two weeks principal photography will begin and there is still no real agreement between Paul and Michael about how Tom's journey into the past is to be depicted. While the opening sequence isn't scheduled for filming until the very end of production, still, a decision must be made about it now because whatever way it is to be realized will profoundly affect the style and atmosphere of all that is shot before it.

Paul seems surprised: he had thought they had agreed upon a plan and that the plan was his. But Michael believes in his own "softer, more magical way"—a way that will need preparation: certain platforms may have to be built, for instance, on which Amanda and Laura can be rolled in and out, and Tom himself may need to ride one as the camera circles around him, or as he circles the camera. Whatever concept is chosen, that choice will be evident in the very first moments of the picture, when Tom, having led us to the derelict apartment that was once the family's home in order to let us witness the events that happened there, summons the memories one by one to appear before us: the apartment as it was, Amanda, Laura, the meal that they are eating.

MICHAEL: You see, my idea is that instead of cutting away from him in the broken-down apartment, when he begins to remember the past we—

PAUL: I don't cut, I cross-dissolve.

MICHAEL: But whether you cut or whether you dissolve, it's all the same: you will be losing him from the screen while you change the scenery. I think it is very important that you see him all the time, while around him everything else is changing.

PAUL: All in the same shot?

MICHAEL: It doesn't need necessarily to be complicated.

PAUL: Then how come I feel sphincters tightening that I never even knew I came equipped with?

MICHAEL: What I am suggesting is that while we are moving around him, slowly, slowly, while we are still on him, we see little pieces of Amanda, or the picture of the father, or the glass menagerie, maybe out of focus even, slide into the frame and out, maybe just past his face, and this bleeding in of things from the past will make it seem more fluid, more easy than if you just go suddenly from present to past with a cross-dissolve or a cut. And while we keep moving around him, we change the light so it gets darker and darker. Then a little bit at a time we put some furniture into the room while the camera is looking in another direction, and maybe we even slide some people in, so when we come around him again we will see more of the past. Each time we go around and come back you will see more, and you keep sliding past him, and in the back you see Amanda sliding in, or the other way Laura is sliding out, and so memory comes back, gradually, softly,

softly, and then finally you are in the past, and all that he is remembering has come together in front of your eyes!

As he talks, and the images swirl down upon each other ever more thickly, the warier Paul grows, for this sounds far more ambitious than his own original concept where transformations would be made in separate shots and later welded optically at the lab into a sequence that would appear seamless only in the final film. He voices profound concern that the technology and timing of a shot like that might be so dazzling in its wizardry as to overwhelm the humanity of the performance and prevent the audience from ever entering the story.

PAUL: It's awesome. It's brilliant. It's *2001*. But all I wanted was a camera that followed like a dog and would be the confessor he spoke to at the exorcism. I wanted to introduce the characters simply, not in order of appearance necessarily because the monologue doesn't deliver them that way, but to reveal them simply—

MICHAEL: I am showing you a way how you can reveal them—

PAUL: But you'd need a set like *Cleopatra*'s to do a shot like that. Miniatures. Special effects. If we sense *machinery* behind it, we're through! It has to be simple. That's why I'm even thinking of resorting to superimposition: let Tom just move into blackness as he walks, and bring up a face out of the past in the limbo behind him till it gradually fills the screen, then, as we pick him up again someplace else, we let it hover there in his memory a minute until it gives way to another—

MICHAEL: What I am telling you is much more magical.

PAUL: I'm also concerned because I don't want the memory to

seem "outside his head." The people, the furniture, are all
things outside his head! The minute they're that solid,
that tangible, and you can see them floating by on circle
dollies, they won't seem like memory anymore.

MICHAEL: It's not as elaborate as what you are thinking. I'm
even hoping at the end to use the same circle dolly again,
so we can come out of the past as softly as we go in. Really,
I can show you on the set. We can work together on the
monitor and I will show you.

PAUL: All right, my darling, you know I never dismiss anything
you say. So you go away and come back with something you
can prove is simple, and while you're gone I'll just take my
clothes off and wait on the couch. I may not always be
eager, but I'm available.

Long after the picture has ended Paul will confide: "I can't
believe we could ever have really set up what Michael wanted. It
would have taken four days and ninety men. You can't start with
an abandoned shell of an apartment and transform it in front of
your eyes into the kind of richly textured place that people live
in, let alone have characters sliding in and out, and furniture
materializing, and pictures appearing on walls, and do all that
while you're making a single shot! Just to do it the *other* way
took a goddam night! Just to take everything *out* of that apartment, and smash the windows and mess up the walls!"

I'm reminded of an argument Paul and I had on *Rachel,
Rachel,* when he challenged the way I had written a scene:
Rachel, in bed, becomes for a moment the child she was and
then transforms into herself again, without cutting away or
stopping the camera. Paul found that with the help of a hinged
wall and a stalwart crew to lift Joanne out of bed and slip her
child-self in while the camera strayed up with her hands to show

family pictures on the wall above her, Paul could stage the most effective transition in the picture nearly as described in the script, but that stunt required only the removal and return of an actress and the intervening substitution of a child, not the metamorphosis of an entire set.

The conversation with Michael seems deadlocked. Neither man has anything further to say. Then Michael takes a breath and smiles at Paul:

MICHAEL: May I ask one other thing? When we go on location next week to shoot the prologue, I would like to do it at the "magic hour," at twilight, or maybe even dawn, so when we follow him inside for his monologue it is already beginning to be dark. What do you say?

PAUL: What I say, Michael, and it may come as a terrible shock, is that I don't—entirely—disagree.

They smile and become quiet over their coffee. They watch the caterers arrive to clear away the crumbs and wilt of yesterday's buffet, including my grenade of a bagel, and to lay clean cloths and arrange fresh platters. It is nearly nine.

Joanne comes in sneezing, but otherwise healed: perhaps out of concern that Paul might be too lonely having a cold all by himself, she now has the beginnings of one too—a lalapalooza, runaway hit of a cold, to judge from the sound of it. Accompanying her on leashes, and pulling her in opposite directions, are Harry, most recent in a line of amiable wirehaired fox terriers whom Paul likes to swing by their jaws from a leather bone, and all of whom have met with tragic ends, and Spanky, the miniature schnauzer, who barks at you no matter how often she's met you. A moment later John arrives, late because his wife left town and took the alarm clock with her. Paul takes him on a walk around the room, speaking to him in that people-proof voice I hate when I'm trying to listen. I think he's telling him how much he wants to set his moves now, while still giving him some leeway to explore, and John is listening with that simian attention and shrugging in what I take to be qualified agreement. As they drift closer to me, stopping every few steps to face each other in another miniconference, I can hear Paul say that he hasn't decided yet whether or not to cut out the interior monologues, one of which begins the scene they plan to rehearse today.

PAUL: . . . I'm not concerned about setting movement in a monologue, that's simple. What I'm concerned about in the monologues is not making them a speech. You have to have an attitude about them, they can't be neutral, they can't be casual. . . .

Out of hearing again, they circle the room and return.

PAUL: . . . and ask us into your head in those monologues the way you'd invite a lady into your room, simply by looking at her in a certain way. You get her attention. Get ours! You've got more than just "things up your sleeve"—pretend you've got the best locker-room joke in the world and you can't wait to tell it. Give it internal importance. Make us hear you. Entice us to hear you. . . .

Their walk ends on the far side of the room. John crosses to the "fire escape" and climbs on top of the chair that represents a ladder on the set. Mary Bailey takes out her stopwatch and the Annunciation scene begins.

JOHN: "Across the alley was the Paradise Dance Hall. Evenings in spring they'd open all the doors—"

PAUL: Relish it. Dine on the poetry. Love the words.

It seems to me he does. Joanne comes out to join him, sitting just below him on an apple box meant to be a windowsill. Over her shoulder, just as Joanne's own mother might have taught her to do as a child, Amanda wishes on that "little silver slipper of a moon" just rising over Garfinkle's Delicatessen. The scene, with its teasing and parrying, its coy evasions, its somehow seductive withholding, is the only joyous mother-and-son scene in the play and provides a hopeful glimpse at a relationship that might have been, if the world had been different and had certain private calamities never happened. Tom tells his mother that he has triumphed in his quest for a gentleman caller and that one will be coming tomorrow night. Thrilled, giddy, fluttering with "plans and preparations," Amanda constructs in her mind a vision of a paragon who will be savior to them all, until Tom reminds her gently of the facts: "I didn't tell him anything about Laura. I just said, 'How about coming home for dinner sometime?' and he said 'Fine,' and that was the whole conversation."

An idea strikes Joanne: to split her focus between the part of her that listens to Tom's description of the gentleman caller and the part that is already sprucing up the rooms in her mind for his arrival, "finding things to hide other things under, like antimacassars for the cigarette burns on the couch."

PAUL: That's just what I wrote down in my script to show you. You want to see?

JOANNE: I believe! I believe!

PAUL: Do it!

Joanne bends down and does something or other in front of an imaginary cupboard. She appears to be digging potatoes. Paul watches with amused curiosity.

PAUL: What are you doing?

JOANNE: Looking for a tablecloth. Can't you tell?

PAUL: In what?

JOANNE: I don't know—isn't there supposed to be some piece of furniture here?

PAUL: You are digging through the phonograph for a tablecloth.

JOANNE: Well, maybe that's where I keep it!

PAUL: Try the upstage wall.

She passes down the lane of tape to where the upstage wall will be. She has to call out her lines to John, who still lounges on the fire escape. Paul likes the effect of it, the distance between them, their independent activities, the discordant rhythms.

PAUL: I really hate to impose this kind of—

He is staring suddenly, like a seer on a blasted heath. Is this some vagary of the mind? What vision is this? What's happening here? He seems to have embarked on a Kazan transition whose destination only he can guess. I follow his gaze:

Harry, the wirehaired terrier, has gotten the scent, or is pretending he's gotten it, of some *thing* under the floor. He is panting rapidly, just this side of cardiac arrest, emitting small canary chirps of recognition as he tries to burrow down through the hardwood like the Count of Monte Cristo digging out of the Chateau d'If, figuring perhaps that if Joanne can create imaginary tablecloths in imaginary phonographs, he can do imaginary rats.

PAUL: Time out. Let us learn from Dog. Now *that* is an example of "actor's intention"!

They all laugh, admiring how surpassingly like a terrier this little terrier is, how his art springs from himself, how he uses his own experience. They return to their own scene and John presents an idea: he recalls a production in which, just before Tom left for the movies, he noticed his own reflection in the mirror and paused to fix his hair. It seems to him a wonderful way to dramatize Tom's self-absorption, especially since it comes so abruptly on the heels of his tender warning to Amanda not to expect too much from the gentleman caller because Laura is "very different from other girls."

PAUL: Show me.

JOHN: See, I think there's something really spooky about it—that he sees himself in the mirror and his whole concern for Laura disappears. I think there are two things: (*a*) he's sad because of all this talk of Laura, but (*b*) he has a date, and he has the presence of mind to remember it and check himself out in the mirror. I think if he's just discombobulated enough—I mean, Amanda has said, "You're a prick and I know you're a prick, but at least have the smallest amount of dignity more than your father did, and don't abandon us!" I mean, she has said some pretty scary things to him, things he never faced, and he's scared because she's right. Especially about his being selfish, but I think he has a really good suspicion that he's not going to do much about that—

PAUL: Except what he did this once: bringing the gentleman caller home. Now he can tell himself he's done all he could and leave with a clear conscience.

JOHN: Yes. Get out. And so in the middle of talking about how Amanda shouldn't expect too much because Laura's not like other girls, he sees himself in the mirror and forgets all about her.

PAUL: Do it.

He does, then does it quickly again. The second time, his discovery of his reflection comes almost by chance, and suddenly. He has to put his glasses on to see if it's really he, and then to assess how attractive he looks with them on and off. He takes them off, puts them on, takes them off, and, making his date important just by the care he takes in his appearance, decides against them finally, puts them back in his pocket, and smooths down his hair. Joanne runs over to straighten his collar, but he leaves before she can. I think it's wonderful—he has even let me know it's a first date! Paul says, "Overelaborate," and wants John to try it without eyeglasses at all, and John does. It seems sterile to me after what I have just seen, and I tell Paul so. "You're baroque," is all he says.

JOHN: The other day you said, "Tom's never bored," but I think he's incredibly bored. I think he's a spoiled little shit. I think he's amused by her—but just sometimes—and that's all, and I think that what communicated last time was boredom with the *scene*.

PAUL: It was so dismissive I didn't even see why the scene went on.

JOHN: Well, I'm trying not to be bored. Was it too bored today, or was it better today? Did I give too much? Because I can play it like that, or even more so.

PAUL: It was fine today.

JOHN: Really fine?

PAUL: Really fine. You can even add to it. That's a nice moment
    with the mirror.

John seems unable to cope with the energy the compliment
gives him so he grabs Michael Ballhaus by the face and spins
him around to show everybody:

JOHN: Isn't this a face that ought to be Tom's father? I mean,
    isn't this a face that would run away?

He drops Michael, who is flushed by the attention, to say
nothing of the power in John's hand. Karen and Jim arrive and
greet Joanne before she retires to the lunch-hour quiet of her
dressing room. There is a lightness in her today, as though she'd
spent the whole night washing out the sky. The three stand
chatting together, and laughing, the old Williamstown brigade. John and Michael are off by themselves, trying to figure
out what Tom means when he says, "I have tricks in my pocket,
I have things up my sleeve" in his first monologue. Paul drifts
over to them, eating his sandwich.

JOHN: Well, *how* is he a magician? How does he bring "truth in
    the pleasant disguise of illusion"? In the play the magic
    was just that I set the stage, that's all—that was the
    magic. That I conjured up the stage picture, and the lights
    came up, and the people I was remembering were there.
    But in this, what's the magic? Is it what I make the camera
    do? That I make it see things that aren't there? Or make
    the scenery appear and disappear? Do I do tricks? Did
    somebody say I've got stuff on my finger that I can set on
    fire without burning myself?

PAUL: You'll have stuff on your finger but not to do tricks. We have to know you'll be able to light the match at the end of that first long dolly shot, so we'll glue sandpaper on your thumb and you won't have to rely on your thumbnail.

JOHN: But what's the magic?

PAUL: That's what Michael and I were discussing this morning, and I just don't want to astonish the audience with conjure tricks. In that long dolly shot we'll explore the derelict apartment as you look all around it. Then when you look the second time, we'll become aware of fragments—a voice that's simply adrift—some fragment of song—some light falling on a piece of glass—a face, maybe superimposed. My resistance is to doing something tricky and technical—

JOHN: In other words you won't actually see that with the camera when I'm there? Because that's all I want to know. I just want to know what I'll be talking about in that monologue.

PAUL: Well, probably what you *won't* see is people sliding by in very well-contrived pools of light over somebody's shoulder.

JOHN: Fine. End of conversation.

"I think what we've got here is a failure to communicate," is what I write, and Paul, looking over my shoulder, mumbles, "A triple failure." I cannot guess how much, or whether at all, Michael has shared with John the differences he is having with Paul about the whole memory question, but John seems disturbed by it now too.

They run the prologue to the Gentleman Caller scene as a

warm-up after lunch, with Amanda's heartbreaking "Jonquils" speech. Joanne has a way of summoning into her eyes such delicious private images of Amanda's past life that I find myself grinning at whatever it is I see sparkling there that she isn't telling. To get her to physicalize the approach of an imminent storm and her concern that the gentleman caller might get caught in it before he can get here, Paul sends Joanne rushing out onto the fire escape to see "how the clouds are piling up." At another point, he stops to take Karen aside and asks her not to dramatize her anxiety about the advent of Mr. O'Connor by fluttering quite so much: "Breathe," he coaches her, "simply breathe. Quickly, with the tops of your lungs, till you hyper-ventilate, then hide it by backing up one step at a time till you're out of the room." Karen tries but it feels "outside herself" and she cannot make it her own; the result is mechanical, so Paul abandons it. Now he's asking Joanne to "sing sweetly" her command for Laura to answer the door, in order to mask from the gentleman caller's ears her irritation with her daughter for her panicky reluctance to let him in.

PAUL: Joanne. Stay upstage when you sing that out.

JOANNE: But I have to come down to get her to answer that bell.

PAUL: Well, don't stand there and point. You look like Brunhilde!

JOANNE: Well, she sang too!

They continue with the scene. Jim Naughton, clearing his throat, finally makes his entrance. So does Spanky, the little gray schnauzer. If Harry can act, so can she! As the gentleman caller is introduced, Spanky wags her rear, not having much tail, then drops a biscuit on his shoe and begins to eat it. When

Amanda charms her visitor onto the couch, Spanky comes too, assisted now by Harry, who trots over for a brief, friendly hump against Jim's knee before trotting back to join his imaginary rats. But after a while, not getting enough attention, he decides to perform his "Watch-how-I-spin-on-my-ass" trick, solemnly and rhythmically revolving himself in a perfect circle around that anatomical point by means of his front paws alone, while at the same time wearing an expression that can only be described as "most professional," although it is hard to imagine one of his breed looking much of anything else. All the actors, led by Jim, pick up Harry's rhythm by humming a slow, accompanying waltz.

JIM: Is he trying to screw himself into the floor?

PAUL: Somebody get him a trailer hitch, quick, before he disappears!

JOHN [*with a certain reverence*]: I think we should whisper. I certainly hope it feels as good as it looks.

The actors and Harry go on with their separate scenes, and when Paul gives his notes at the end, Harry's right there.

PAUL: Well, it's got some good stuff in it. John, as a gesture of hope against all odds that something might happen for Laura tonight, when Amanda calls you to supper, take the bottle of beer out of Jim's hand before you come in the house. And Jim, while you're on the couch and Amanda's telling you white lies about how domestic Laura is, make a mental note: "Aha! They brought me here for something!" Find the moment. Also, Jim—at the table: it's nifty when you smile! Just nifty!

They attempt to begin again, but since Harry's circus act everything has made Joanne laugh, and Jim doesn't help matters any by inviting Spanky to sit at the table with them, where the little dog remains throughout the "meal." Perhaps to get serious, Joanne moves to the attack and switches attention suddenly to all of us: "The people who are watching against that white wall are just like an audience and it's making me play everything straight out front!" We scramble out of her way as though a runaway truck had come at us, Michael whipping his chair into a corner while I whip mine to the vicinity of the buffet, where I hope my balding head will somehow blend in with the grapes.

They reach the end of the play for the first time. "Go to the moon, you selfish dreamer!" Amanda cries after her escaping son. And John gives his final soliloquy, ending with, "For nowadays the world is lit by lightning! Blow out your candles, Laura—and so, goodbye." After two days the run-through is over. Is this all there is to it? It has felt unplayed, unclimactic somehow, and I realize that at no point have I felt "transported." Am I expecting too much at this stage of rehearsal? Why do I feel this flatness? I think of the last line in *Rachel, Rachel,* when the schoolteacher, played by Joanne, leaves Manawaka for the last time and muses on the bus that bears her away, "What will happen? What will happen?"

The day ends so abruptly it takes me by surprise. Paul is off to Atlanta again and has left without goodbyes. I've made no plans for the evening and I feel depressed. I have that inexpressible hurt feeling I used to get in high school when I'd leave to walk to the subway alone, too fast for anyone to follow, and feel as if they'd walked away from me.

Seventh
Day of
Rehearsal

Paul bounds in, freshly back from Road Atlanta where, with the rainy malfunctions of last weekend behind him, he has put his car on the pole for next week's race. While vibrating with good feelings about his success, he tries to persuade me at the same time that he is actually filled with "a wistful melancholy" because this week's Actors Studio premiere of *The Color of Money* has forced him to confront the fact that the picture is over, and with it all the fun and camaraderie he had enjoyed in the process of making it. Now he can only look back with fondness on an experience he hoped would never end.

I have just cracked my head on the bottom of a shelf as I rose abruptly away from a cake pan. Paul says, "Either stay away from that cake or pull out that nail. You'll drive it right through your brain." But observing that this is the third morning in a row I have had the same accident, he decides that warnings are no longer enough, so after trying and failing several times in the last few minutes to pull out the nail himself, he is now industriously crosshatching masking tape into a pad that will cover the shelf. I wonder sometimes if I find such normal human consideration in him remarkable only because he's a star. I wonder who picked out his wardrobe today. Terry cloth socks of Day-Glo pink! One of the dogs might have pulled them out of the washer.

Leaving the room lights on, they attack the Gentleman Caller scene, first on the schedule today. I watch Karen. Her questions to Mr. O'Connor are monotone and hoarse, like one of the hearing-handicapped who have never heard human speech, and she has given Laura a chronic depression. She lapses into blankness whenever the gentleman caller speaks, coming out of it just too late to hear what he says. She seems always just a fraction out of step, as though her mind were limping too. How odd it seems, and how effective! The actual limp, though improved, remains unconvincing.

Rehearsal seems endless today. The room boils. The radiators bang like marching bands. My eyelids droop in the heat. The actors keep vanishing even as I stare at them, leaving black holes in the air where they have been sitting, the way visiting lecturers used to do in those vast Victorian meeting halls at college when the evening went on too long. I look over at Paul. He's frowning as he watches their work. I try to guess what he's thinking and whether he plans to help. I imagine myself shouting, "For God's sake, people, stop! It's empty! What's wrong?" and for a moment in my dozing I think I have. But nobody's looking this way; I'm not in disgrace. I'm nodding again. "Too quiet out there, bwana." "Well, that's Africa." Harry Carey in *Trader Horn,* or was it *Tarzan?* The Capitol Theatre. I'm there with my father, fifty-five years ago on a Saturday morning.

Johnny Weissmuller, in person, coming down on a vine from the flies, and diving into a glass-fronted tank to swim. I jolt awake. Paul still waits, letting them spin out their discoveries and fall on their mistakes like swords. I wonder how he has the patience, no matter what he says about knowing from scraps of evidence that they'll all come through in the end, not to intervene.

PAUL: You're anticipating the end of the scene, so you have nowhere to go. The flowers are already open. You're too quiet inside, it's too easy for you both. I want to see self-deception at the beginning, Jim, and your terrified disconnection, Karen, and I don't want to see them at the end.

JIM: I guess what you also don't want to see is that I came out here to do a scene for twenty minutes. The problem I have is when I try to do your note, "Be all wrapped up in yourself," it makes me more reflective than I should be.

PAUL: Maybe you can be wrapped up in yourself *louder.* Love remembering more. High school, her, Blue Roses, singing in *The Pirates of Penzance.* Love *yourself* for remembering! The way you loved yourself for singing the song, remembering how great you were in *The Pirates of Penzance,* then making a big, loud joke of it so she doesn't catch you feeling, by getting up and singing the rest *loud!*

JIM: What's the objective in the scene? To make her feel good.

PAUL: But how skilled are you at that? If you're too good at the beginning, there's no scene. Nothing should work. You have to come into a hospital room where somebody's dying and say, "So what's new?"

KAREN: I find the more he pays attention to me, the more I withdraw.

PAUL: Jim, sell yourself even more. Solosexual. Let it have nothing to do with her, which will be terrific, but don't let it *look* that way. Don't sell hard, sell muted. Not purple and red: violet and pink.

JIM: Violet and pink—I'll have to chew on that awhile.

PAUL: Even selling should have a kind of patina over it. Karen, you've encased her in too much Oriental remoteness—it's not jerky enough anymore, it's too contained. Hide. Hide. Keep edging your cushion back. The kiss was first-rate. I won't tell you most of what I really liked: you'd keep trying to recapture what you did instead of creating it. The one way you can really kill a performance is to tell the actor what you thought was great.

Jim tells a theatre story: an old actress has come backstage to give some advice to an ingenue after the matinee: "You must always remember to ask for the *tea,* my dear, not for the *laugh."*
They lapse into silence, thinking hard.

KAREN: It's a big decision to tell him I was the girl in the leg brace. It didn't seem difficult in the play. I keep thinking I ought to make it difficult—

PAUL: Make it easy till after you've done it, then take it back without taking it back, and that will make it difficult.

KAREN: Hmm.

They try the scene again. Karen is better, but Jim's heart isn't in it. A moment ago he put the candelabrum on the floor without bothering first to see if there was any other place to put it down and made the whole scene appear prearranged. Anticipation again, the thing good actors scoff at, and he's annoyed at himself for falling into it. Something's distracting him. He isn't truly here. Paul lets it go on awhile, then stops him.

PAUL: Pay attention to how physical positions feel to you. Anything that feels right is wrong. "I'm as comfortable as a cow" works because you don't look comfortable. Leaning in on your elbow is intimate, so if you do it when you say, "I hope you don't think I'm getting personal," it's right because it's wrong. If you back away physically from the intimacy, it's wrong because it's right. I hand out revolvers in case this bewilders anybody. I know what I'm trying to say, but I'm saying it badly.

What I hear is not connecting with the right side of my brain: it sounds technical, external. I admire it, I can follow it, and as an actor I could never do it. After lunch they run the scene again, this time by candlelight. I get a sudden notion that I keep to myself: what if the gentleman caller, who has had a big day at the warehouse, were to fall asleep during one of his own speeches, so Laura's "Mr. O'Connor, have you kept up with your singing?" could really be said in order to wake him up so he could talk to her some more?

A shift in the atmosphere breaks into my musing: the gentleman caller has just kissed Laura and is backing away to observe his effect on her. Karen stands with her eyes shut, shimmering. Paul whispers to her from the edge of the candlelight, "Don't know it's his only kiss." She takes it in, then begins to tremble with expectancy, a little girl wearing a blindfold, her face tilted toward Jim, following his warmth, her lips parted gently by desire, asking for more, holding on to the afterglow of his kiss as hard as she can, transforming behind her closed eyes from the child she was to the woman she is, possessor of a secret now that no one can take away. But no second kiss follows. "Open your eyes," Paul coaches, wanting her to see what he sees: the gentleman caller is putting on his jacket. Then, as Mr. O'Connor explains that he can't see her anymore because he's engaged, Karen, without moving at all, shrinks back into the invalidism of Laura—numbly, sweetly, generously, and without reproach. She gives Mr. O'Connor the wounded unicorn, and I feel along with him the full blow of the tragedy, for Jim Naughton makes it theirs, not Laura's alone, an astonishing accomplishment. It's as though, in this scene of nonconnection, they had stumbled together into a well they hadn't known was there, and discovered during their fall a connection too promising to survive, and what a chance for redemption is lost! For the first time I realize how very near the edge of healing the play is allowed to come before it crashes and kills everyone aboard.

PAUL: Nice work, guys. Not uninteresting at all.

We break for the weekend. A relaxed trip in the limo with Paul and Michael, to view the special effects of candlelight and the makeup tests at the Fifty-fifth Street lab. Michael has been trying out different filters and film stocks: Kodak's "more contrasty" look for the colder scenes of the present, and Agfa's warmer tones for the scenes of memory. We get caught in a traffic gridlock near the Fifty-ninth Street Bridge: two stubborn cars have checkmated each other at an intersection, and simply stopped New York. Paul sighs:

PAUL: One of these days I'm going to have them build me a stretch limousine a hundred and fifty feet long, so long it'll take four traffic lights to get it past an intersection—a stretched-out Volkswagen Rabbit is what I want. Gridlock the gridlockers; detonate the bastards!

Michael laughs convulsively, then lets go a series of little afterchuckles as each of the day's tensions departs.

The lights in the screening room dim and in the dark close-ups appear of our four principal players wearing only the tops of their costumes: Karen looking freckled and tanned; Jim younger and handsomer than in life, his dark eyes mischievous but watchful; John in his Merchant Marine pea coat and stocking cap, pale and extremely serious; and then Joanne, with that opalescent skin that takes on the colors of anything near it, animated, chattering away with someone just off camera, not willing to waste a second if there's something to share. I can't hear a word she's saying because the film's without sound, but I guffaw loudly in appreciation. Paul, not understanding, and instantly protective of her, barks his displeasure: "Why are you laughing?" "Because she's so—*Joanne,*" I say, and he sees the joke too and lets it go. "That cap hugs John like a cloche," he complains. "We ought to roll it back on his head." The lights come up. Paul doesn't want makeup on anyone, so Michael will see if black lace filters will do the trick.

"You're not coming to dinner?" Paul asks once we're down in the street. "I don't know—am I supposed to?" We are driven to the apartment house on Fifth and find Joanne propped up in her four-poster sickbed, red-nosed and clogged but having a wonderful time. Books, half-written letters, and knitting surround her, and a steam kettle whistles away. All she can do is sleep, she says with the kind of yawn you'd only show to a friend, and reminds Paul that besides the remains of the fried chicken in the fridge there's caviar. She gives me her *Tosca* tickets for Monday night at the Met and wants to fix me up with my mother, to which I agree.

Paul sets the table in the terrace solarium while I dish out fried chicken and salad in the kitchen. We light candles and he opens the wine. The city rising above the park is dazzling tonight, and the reservoir below us glows like a sapphire. I can see from far downtown all the way north to the bend in the Hudson above the George Washington Bridge. The candles on the table remind me of the ones we just saw on the screen, candles for the Gentleman Caller scene designed to shed extraordinary light: they fit over aluminum cores in which bulbs are concealed to shine up at the faces of the actors, and the wires attached to their bases flow out through the candelabrum, down Jim's sleeve, and are plugged into outlets on the floor. Paul has made toast for the caviar, of which there must be half a pound, and we eat it like marmalade. Dining slowly, crunching our chicken bones, drinking in the view, and getting mellow on a wine of such quality that I don't even bother to look at the label, we talk. "Nice," he says, looking at the silhouette of the city. "Nice." We talk of friendship, but our speech is getting mushy; we talk of ourselves. He tells me he's never made a decision in his life—it's been all dumb luck and irresponsibility. "Bullshit!" is my rejoinder, as I bang the table and miss. "You take *risks!*" He shakes his head. "You can only take credit for risking if the risks are calculated," he says, orating a little. "If they're the whimsical products of irresponsibility and recklessness they aren't risks. They're just things that turn out or don't turn out." "No! *Risks!*" I holler. "Like this *movie!*" It goes on like that, getting nowhere, and he has to get to bed.

We hug good night at the door, banging each other on the back for about five minutes like a couple of seals applauding, and I manage to wish him well for the big race in Atlanta this weekend. I bump into the doorjamb going out, and on the way down in the elevator I think, "Is it really thirty-three years that I've known him? Thirty-five more, I'll be a hundred."

Taps.

Eighth
Day of
Rehearsal

A moment ago Paul strode into the rehearsal hall trying to hide his grin, but now everyone's crowding around him to shake hands. Except John, who's sitting apart from the others on a tall director's chair. While the Mets were losing yesterday, Paul was winning at Road Atlanta, his fourth national championship and his second in a row at that track. "Not bad for an old man," he says, accepting congratulations. He and his pal, Jim Fitzgerald—who held more championships than any other racer in the Sports Car Club of America when he died—had joked about Atlanta's dangerous long downhill right turn: Fitzie said it always gave him butterflies, and laughed when Paul called it "The Ho-hum." Joanne is still "flu-ish," Paul tells us, and on her way to see her doctor, so he'd like Karen and Jim to work in their dressing rooms while he goes through the monologues with John. "And then," he says, throwing an arm around Michael Ballhaus, "we will have a walk-through of the whole movie for the benefit of our Prussian's Prussian eye." But no one leaves. They linger at the buffet, chatting about *Tennessee Williams' South* on PBS last night, in which Jim played Tom in a scene from *The Glass Menagerie*. The play switches partners more frequently than *La Ronde*.

Paul is talking earnestly with John now, who still hasn't budged from his chair. He's full of secret smiles today, and a kind of wonder that makes him appealing. He has a weekend's growth of beard in anticipation of Friday's shoot at the Harlem tenement, and he still hasn't yielded up his curlicue. Paul is trying to find a tactful way to set his moves for the opening monologue, and over the chitchat at the buffet I can hear him saying: "Restlessness! Explosion! Find something to force it!" while John listens, giving nothing away. After a few minutes everyone leaves and we have the room to ourselves.

PAUL: John, I think when he says his father "fell in love with long distance" is the first time we find out that Tom drinks. He should have a little flask—

JOHN [*producing one from his pocket*]: I've got this.

PAUL: Fine. Now invite the camera. Do whatever you can to make it follow. Michael, watch this.

But John delivers the opening monologue in the same flat, stilted way he did at the first reading, full of schoolboy *a*'s and *e*'s followed by those crevasse-confronting hesitations. But this time when he mentions his father, he takes a decorous nip from his flask, a nip of such breeding it makes him Amanda's son even before we meet her, then he toasts the spot on the wall where, in memory, his father's picture hangs. The monologue ends.

JOHN: Was the sense of confession there?

PAUL: Yes, but it's casual. Sharpen it. The beats all need definition. I don't care what it is, but they have to have color. When you mention "in Spain there was revolution" and when you mention "Guernica," I like the wryness. But the way you say your first two lines can invalidate the whole movie if your voice goes up at the ends of those sentences. They won't seem important. This has to be important, important enough to make you *demand* our attention, *demand* that the *camera* pays attention, and you don't command by ending a sentence on a question. You brought us here to listen to your confession. That's not a very pleasant thing to witness, so you have to *demand* it!

John tries again but the difference seems minuscule. Is he rebelling, after all, and if he is, what makes him do it? Is he resisting what Paul wants? His sentences, to my ear, aren't questions really, but they have an evenness to them, a softness, and the images come so quickly the effect is tentative and light. Once in a while he pauses to give emphasis and I find myself momentarily intrigued. But there seems something perfunctory about it, something veiled and uncommitted. All at once he explains just what he's doing:

JOHN: You want confession, but the thing about confession is that it's reticent and shy. So the *ways* of confession are at odds with the obligation to *tell* the story, to *command* attention.

PAUL: Having the camera there will help—ordering it to hear you. "Get your ass in here right now, I want you to get this on film!" The energy may be superficial, but it will help.

Paul seems not to have heard what John said. John smiles. Why, when he's so irreproachably cooperative and pleasant, do I continue to sense some secret mutiny? Is that slight, mocking smile his own, or is it Tom's? It's difficult to tell, with actors of this quality, where characterization leaves off and life begins. Tom Wingfield would surely mock Paul's direction, just as he mocks his mother's "Chew! Chew! Chew!"—in secret. Is John Malkovich even at this rehearsal, or does he only arrive as the clockwork inside Tom, reacting as Tom all day, until he goes home? Under his chic, bloused, raspberry shirt is a bruiser's body, and it didn't surprise me the other day when he told us of chasing a purse snatcher at night, not *out* of Central park but *into* it! There's danger under that shirt, and it gives him suspense. As Tom, with that tearose-velvet voice he has found, and those slightly crossed blue eyes, and that shambling gravedigger's gait, he gives off a deeply distancing atmosphere. He seems to need nobody. He's like a Basque shepherd, or some solitary clamdigger on a sandbar off the coast of Maine.

Michael comes forward at the end of the monologue.

MICHAEL: It's a complicated thing to time.

PAUL: How tightly do we have to strap him into his movements?

MICHAEL: It depends which way you do it. We can move around him a lot while he moves a little in a circle, or we can stay inside the circle while he moves a lot.

PAUL: Maybe we should get some stand-ins to walk it. What's happening on the set right now?

MICHAEL: They are painting, but anyhow I can take you there. I can show you where the camera could be.

PAUL: Let's do it at lunch.

MICHAEL: It would be nice at least to decide the opening shot, if it's his point of view or not—

PAUL: At lunch.

John is running through his second monologue when Joanne arrives. We hear her before we see her, spreading news to people in the hall: "According to the *New York Times* this morning," she is saying, "it has now been definitely proven that inhaling other people's smoke is just as dangerous as smoking yourself, and that's probably why I'm sick." It's her nice way of saying, "No Smoking at Rehearsal." Her cold is in remission, but she's still as hoarse as a crow. Karen and Jim come in with her, having been summoned from upstairs.

PAUL: From the top of the play—let's just walk it for positions. Joanne, save your voice.

I whisper to Mary Bailey that some of the heads that bothered Joanne are back against the same wall, and she goes to route them to the other side of the room. Joanne plays in whispers at first, but as she warms to her opening scene the voice returns and by the time she reaches those seventeen gentlemen callers, she's in full cry. Paul watches, straddling his Porgy chair, sunglasses hanging from his ear, industriously biting his nails.

PAUL [*as they finish the scene*]: Needs compression.

Suddenly he suggests that during Amanda's soliloquy Tom should remain at the open door, blowing smoke onto the fire escape, until he hears her reach "that beautiful, brilliant young Fitzhugh boy" in her catalog of suitors, and then come alert and reveal to us, by the interest that brings him back into the room, a first hint of his homosexuality.

John listens to Paul without a flicker of expression, goes to write the ideas down in his script, then wanders over to stand behind Karen, who's sitting at her typewriter, dreaming, and suddenly starts typing from behind her, his arms encircling her and his chin on top of her head. It's the most intimate I've seen him be with anyone, the most protective, the most brotherly, and somehow it moves me very deeply.

The run-through goes on. In the Deception scene, when Joanne hurries in to confront Laura about her truancy from typing school, I count sixteen separate fingers as she panto-mimes peeling off her gloves, and nine imaginary hatpins fly out of her hat, some of them straight in her eye. She tends to be careless about where she puts objects she's only pretending, and often loses count, and I realize how much she means it when she says "all that sense-memory stuff at acting school" never meant a thing to her. She knows perfectly well that when the real props arrive she'll know how to deal with them superbly, just as Bea Lillie knew from the start that there was never any point in "playing" a rehearsal because it was always her audience that cued her comic timing. But I wish I had those sixteen-fingered gloves.

Paul stands at ease, all the angles of his body falling gracefully into opposition, like a plate from *How to Draw the Perfect Human Figure*. I see dotted lines angling from all his joints. As the scene ends, he applauds and laughs.

PAUL: Karen! A wonderful thing! You flicked your hair out of your eyes without having the hair to flick. What a wonder-ful gesture of dismissal. Find ten or twelve places to do that. Joanne! Too much of everyone else. Not enough of The Lady.

JOANNE: "Everyone else" *who?*

PAUL: The kids, the dogs, how the hell do I know who you brought in here this morning?

JOANNE [*laughing*]: Oh, they're all here, huh?

She's like moonlight seen through the bottom of a porcelain teacup, not any color at all. Only her watch strap tells you where she is. Drew takes the orders for lunch and we all troop up to the unfinished set so Michael can show Paul his scheme for the first monologue, and so Paul can see whether the Drunk scene plays better on the fire escape, where John and Michael would like it, or on the stairs, where Paul thinks it belongs.

"Michael was very excited," Paul will tell me later, "because the fire escape would get him out of that apartment. He'd have those dance hall lights from across the alley to play with—the texture of brick—the pattern of those ladders. But I pointed out that when Tom comes home it's three or four o'clock in the morning and the dance hall would be closed. John liked the fire escape for another reason: he thought it would be deliciously sneaky if that was his secret way in when he came home drunk at night, and he envisioned an opening for that scene that he thought was marvelous photographically. You'd see him drop his keys, then his silhouette would come skulking past all the windows, and try each one to see if one was open, but I thought the secrecy should be between Tom and his sister, not Tom and his fire escape, and I was afraid that all the intimacy of the scene would vaporize in all that open air, compared to what could happen on that staircase. But I was willing to try it both ways."

Michael leads us to the platform where the set stands. The brightness of raw wood is disappearing under paint, and the rooms look smaller.

MICHAEL: Whatever way you do it, I would like to see candles in the beginning. Laura is waiting for him in the living room with candles, to come home.

PAUL: I think that'll look like a deathwatch.

MICHAEL: So maybe she isn't really waiting so much. Maybe she just has insomnia.

KAREN: Or I'm using the candles to look at my glass menagerie.

MARY BAILEY: Yes, playing with the animals' moods in the candlelight, changing their expressions as she moves them.

KAREN: She's turned the lights out so she won't disturb her mother.

PAUL: It's a trade-off, fellas. If she's waiting for her brother, it's concern. If she's playing with her animals, it's being inside her head. You can't have it both ways.

MICHAEL: Why not? Can't a loving sister play with her animals while she is waiting for her brother to come home?

Paul smiles and shakes his head. He opens the door to the stairwell that leads down one short flight to the stage, and lets the actors pass through. Before he can follow, Michael pulls him back to discuss his own priority: how he wants to film the monologue. Soon I hear Karen and John on the stairs rehearsing the Drunk scene by themselves. Michael walks Paul through the shot he has planned, painting with his hands all the elements of his vision, where John will move, where the camera will circle, how the phantoms of the past will be borne in . . .

MICHAEL: . . . and as we come around, gradually it is night, and here we see on the floor some broken glass where used to be the glass menagerie, and here was once the picture of the father—and as we come around and come around, slowly,

slowly, the present turns into the past, and I think it would be nice if we would see the dance hall lights on him, and very dimly you begin to see Amanda and Laura, and here is the menagerie how it was, and so again we come around slowly . . .

John, still deep in his rehearsal of the Drunk scene, comes bursting out of the stairwell into Michael's shot. He stands there panting between Paul and Michael, nearly blocking their view of each other, oblivious to them, working up to his "Goody, goody! Pay 'er back for all those 'Rise an' Shines!'" as Karen rushes in behind him. Paul, oblivious to John, is saying to Michael—as though John weren't standing between them—"If Amanda's here, and if he moves there—" And John, seeing for the first time that he has walked right into the middle of a camera discussion that has nothing to do with the scene, drops Tom back into the waking dream he came from and asks mildly, "What's going on?" Michael, unwilling to let Paul go now that he's got him, won't interrupt himself and hurtles on, trying to quote dialogue as he pretends to be Tom: "And the fifth character in this play is here, my father, who fell in love with long distance—" Paul grins finally, seeing the absurdity of it all, and stops him with a hand.

PAUL: No! No! No! [*imitating Michael*] "Slowly, slowly we pan up! We see strings on John's wrists. His hands begin flapping—bloop! Bloop! And we slowly, slowly continue to pan up, up the strings until we come to a picture frame, and there is the daddy hanging on the wall, only not a picture of him but really the daddy, also played by John of course, and he has all those strings in his hand, and he pulls one—bloop! Up goes John's right hand! Bloop! Up goes the left—"

They laugh. It's all surreal. Layered realities. Time for Alice to shout, "You're nothing but a pack of cards!" and go fleeing down the chessboard and backward through the looking glass. John kidnaps Paul and leads him into the stairwell to watch another rehearsal of the Drunk scene. The stairway is too narrow for observers, so I stay outside, in the bay window of the living room, where I can be out of the way and still write notes from what I hear. John comes bursting up the stairs again, but, never one to visit the same place twice, he practically lands on my lap. "Goody, goody!" he yells out Tom's dialogue, and throws himself into some wild improvisation at Laura's typewriter. My knees are touching the backs of his, my clipboard's in the middle of his back. I freeze, pen poised, eyes lowered in the dumb belief that if I can't see him, he can't see me and what he's doing won't be interrupted. The scene ends and I breathe again. Paul loves what they have given him down there: the narrowness of the stairway conspired with an accident of timing to create a moment he feels could have not been come upon in any other way.

STEWART: What happened? What went on?

PAUL: She was sitting on the step beside him and suddenly got up to leave, and in trying to stop her, so he could play the scene face-to-face, John found himself behind her on the stairs and was forced to play the whole revelation of the magic scarf over her shoulder, with his cheek against hers. He had to put one arm entirely around her to pull the scarf out of his other sleeve, and wave it in front of her, and drape it over her head. Once they found themselves stuck there, they knew instinctively that the accident had put them in a position more intimate than anyone could have planned, and they yielded and didn't correct it, and all of a sudden they were brother and sister, really in contact, and able to show each other their sweetest side. It just happened. It was wonderful!

I remember John typing with his arms around Karen, his chin on her head, and recognize the seed of this moment. Paul turns to John now: "Is it too much, you right up against her like that? Are you worried about it looking like incest?" "That's exactly what I love!" Michael interjects. "The closer the better!" "Ze closer ze besser!" John mimics. "I luff inzest, jah!"

But because he has promised it to them, Paul lets them try the same scene on the fire escape—another set where there is no room for onlookers. "When we tried to put them back in those positions," he tells me later, "it was totally artificial. With John up and down that ladder, all you had was a scene about a fire escape, and I saw the intimacy simply slip very slowly away, so I finally said, 'Back to the stairs! I'm not sacrificing the humanity of this scene to shoot any goddam fire escape.' And that was that."

On our return to the dungeon we pass the stage where Woody Allen is to begin shooting *September* next week. I saw him the other day at the end of his rehearsal, walking very quickly to his limousine and followed by an entourage of what seemed like thirty people, all hurrying after him and handing him things. I never thought of Woody Allen in a limousine, or leading an entourage. He just looked straight ahead, got in, and was driven away. He didn't smile at anyone. Now, Paul goes with limousines, if he can eat popcorn in them. Joanne even more so. But Woody Allen doesn't. He goes with shoes.

Paul is handed his half a tuna sandwich when we reach the rehearsal hall. He goes directly to Michael, turns his back on him, and says, "You're the camera. I'm Tom." He snaps his fingers over his shoulder, feigning Tom's lighting of the match, then turns to make eye contact with Michael as if he were the camera lens, and walks away saying, "I have tricks in my pocket, I have things up my sleeve," luring Michael to dolly after him with the tiniest gesture of invitation, then blowing out the "match" a second later. Michael nods agreement. Suddenly, without any transition at all, Paul is dragging a metal chair across the floor and sitting down by me.

PAUL: Nature or nurture?

STEWART: Beg pardon?

PAUL: Nurturists over here with the Freudians. Naturists over there with the survivalists. Two brothers who've had no nurturing. What is it that makes one brother numb himself completely so he never has to feel pain or loss or rage or ecstasy or anything else, and *survive,* and what makes the other have no defense, feel everything, and be demolished? Same mother. Nature or nurture? Which rules? And why? Should it be war? Should it be two kids living down a manhole in the street? What arena?

I stare at him the way Jim did when Paul said, "Tracing!" Then it dawns on me that he is offering me not another of his koans, but a theme for the basis of a screenplay: it's related to his own mystery, this theme he's giving me, the mystery of his distance from himself, his anesthetized affect, his sense of being forever wistfully apart from both the truly blue-eyed people and the brown, his lost son's anguish, his own "good luck." How to explain them? What shapes us, dooms us, saves us? Nurturing, or the natures we were born with? Freud or genetics? Mama or DNA? And if DNA, why bother with psychiatry? Ever since I wrote *The Rack* for him, out of a gleam in Rod Serling's marvelous eye, Paul has been kidding me for what he calls my

"Daddy never kissed me" scenes, and I've always wondered why he's had to scoff at them when they've provided the basis for some of the loveliest work he has done. Is he trying to invalidate a part of himself that might long, and dread, to believe that it isn't just DNA? Because in that event whom would he blame among his predecessors? And among his successors, who might blame him? When I venture that he seems to be expressing some torment, he says, "Nope, just thought it was interesting," and scrapes his chair away. I sit half in and half out of his trust, like Jim's gentleman caller in his comedy coat.

As I watch the rehearsal go on, I begin to think I'm wrong about John's "mutiny." Maybe what it is with him is just his insistence on the right to protect his process and reserve his plan till he's certain that it's ready to be shown, the right to grow it privately inside. What looks like resistance may only be the way an artist appears when he's husbanding his talent and honoring himself in the only way he knows. You don't process film in a lighted room: what develops in the dark, like what happens between the sheets, may be nobody else's business in the end.

They have moved forward now to the Apology scene. What the scene gains at this rehearsal is a deeper understanding of the power of silence to punish and destroy. Mother and son, both clinging fast to the same weapon, gradually become victimized by their hold on it until it seems impossible for them ever to reach out to each other again. The random click of a cup, an unconscious sigh, the scrape of a chair, all assume painful significance as reminders of the way it used to be when there was the sound of talk in the house, wounding as much of that talk was, so that when John summons the courage to apologize, we see two people as starved to forgive as they are to be forgiven, and pathetically anxious to restore—even temporarily—the only relationship they know how to conduct: their passionate and wretched symbiosis. There's no daylight now between Joanne and Amanda, and John is a different creature: his pallor, his little shrugs, his donkey stamp, his odd, soft, Barbara Walters *r*'s, and all the other elements of character that have been flying around so randomly have come together in this rehearsal like swarms of blackbirds settling on a tree and become one thing. Amanda's suffering for Laura made Joanne cry for the first time. Her hoarseness has returned, and after a day of fighting her swollen throat, she's ready to go home. Paul mixes salt and hot water in a Styrofoam cup, stirs it, and carries it to her to gargle with at the sink with the slimy drain.

PAUL: You should have been doing this all day, not just when you thought of it. Go up to wardrobe and have your fitting, but don't talk to anybody. Then I'll take you home.

She leaves, mouthing her silent good-night, and the day ends with a thump, like a snowball hitting a windshield. I leave too. I have already put on my robe and set out my Chicken Kitchen repast when I remember that I have to get dressed again, ride uptown, take my mother to dinner, and go to hear *Tosca* at the Met.

It turns out to be a graceful evening. She is waiting at the top of the grand stairway when I get there, having climbed up all alone, and at eighty-nine looks ravishing and happy.

Ninth
Day of
Rehearsal

Jim Naughton wanders around our dungeon imitating a trumpet. It is so uncannily real that I have to go over and look down his throat to see if that's really where the sound is coming from; he even makes the *mistakes* trumpeters make when they try for notes they can't reach! Paul arrives and is duly impressed.

PAUL: I can do a tennis match.

He does it all with his mouth and eyes: "Pong-pucka-paw pucka-pong pucka-ping!" I've heard it tried before but never with the sound of the ball hitting the *court,* or bouncing with that dead sound off the rim of a racket. It's the court that's the wonder: clay from the pitch of it. But now too many eyes are on him, so he stops. Before Jim can even put sugar in his tea, Paul calls, "Roll 'em!" plunges the stage into darkness, and relights the ceremonial candles.

I take my accustomed seat near the anteroom door so I can have light to write by. I'm sitting behind Karen, who is turned away from me on a chair with COTTON CLUB stenciled across the back of it, a relic of another film that was shot here. Her narrow form bends forward, hugging itself for protection. Even her hair looks shy. The scale of her performance is better now: less accessible to me unless I seek it, less obvious to the lens that will record it. For the best screen performances are never given. They have to be stolen by us watchers in the dark.

Mary Bailey, who has been substituting gamely for Joanne whenever her throat has kept her away from rehearsals, has dropped Amanda's southern accent today, presumably having given up hope of ever playing the part, and reads the offstage lines in her own shy, woodwind voice. Paul wanders back and forth hugging his shepherd's crook, chasing some dragonfly thought while all of us wait. He stops in front of Jim and says "Uh-h-h" for a rather long time, then changes his mind and walks away. "Let's just dick around," he says, finally. The tapers in Jim's candles need replacing: they've burned down nearly to stubs after all these days and look as if they might not last the scene. Paul stops the run-through almost as soon as it gets started.

PAUL: You're both idling your engines. Get 'em going! Rev 'em up! Don't let yourselves get comfortable. Don't catch each other's rhythms. It's Bach this morning. Let me hear Stravinsky!

They go over and over the scene but it's like trying to skin a hog with a wooden spoon. The morning falls into ruins. The actors deflate. Whatever it was that lay on the scene before the kiss brought it suddenly to life the other day is lying on it again. Paul is talking about things like "energy" and "pace," the externals of performance, while the actors seem to be waiting for something else from him, some saving instruction, organic and visceral, that will reach inside and turn them on like lamps. The feeling that things are wrong and he can't right them preoccupies Jim and makes him anticipate again, and interferes with Karen's "illusion of the first time." They are paddling in fog, around and around. Paul stops them again, but only to offer more mechanics.

PAUL: Jim, get anchored. Get your focus off her and get to the chewing gum quicker. Karen. Too comfortable. The second you get used to one chair, shift to another.

He doesn't want to tell them too much, and he's told me why. It's a difficult scene to enliven when feelings are "down." A character we've never met before, whom Tennessee only describes as generically as peaches that just say "Peaches" on the can, is suddenly plunked down for nearly an act to talk about himself. And the scene's worn ragged by overuse as audition material for student actors. How can anyone play it freshly? Its final minutes had real tragedy yesterday, but how can they be arrived at time after time without some remarkable secret subtext to prepare the way, full of mysterious insinuations? Any scene that is "about what it's about" needs a special golden hammer to make it ring. Rehearsal winds down, ticks, and stops.

PAUL: I'm afraid of improving it into a failure. Let's quit while we're ahead.

KAREN: I've been trying so hard to remember my moves that I'm stuck in mechanics. Could we just *talk* our way through once without moving?

PAUL: How many pages before he sings his pirate song?

MARY BAILEY: Six, I believe.

JIM: Six slo-o-w pages!

KAREN: I wouldn't mind even just *racing* through!

Jim rubs his head savagely, revolves his neck, clears his throat, sings, "Mi mi mi mi mi," and they *do* race through, but as hopelessly as refugees trying to catch a moving train. Paul watches, unperturbed, his outstretched booted feet by the candelabrum in which one of the candles has guttered and gone out. How can he seem so calm? they must wonder. How can he give us so little when we need so much! They don't know what I know: fear of "tampering" makes him refrain. The actors cannot know the certainty he has in them, and he cannot tell them why he's certain without explaining what it will not serve them to hear.

JIM: I'm just indicating. I'm not doing anything at all.

A production assistant comes to take our orders for lunch. "Chow mein," Jim says. We are told that Joanne is in the building. "Good," says Paul.

I escape upstairs to thank her for my *Tosca* tickets and find her sitting in a makeup chair while Tony Walton snaps pictures. Compact, bearded, modest, and immensely gifted and practical, Tony has the eyes of Saint Sebastian after that first flight of arrows, an expression that can only be described as *Innocence Surprised,* full of love and pain and the toughness to endure. Joanne is trying on cloches and sun hats, clowning flirtatiously into the mirror while grilling me about *Tosca*. I am just telling her how the basso dislocated Eva Marton's jaw with a misplaced blow, when Michael beckons her to the makeup tests he's shooting and asks John to join her so he can match his complexion with hers. They have been reshooting his "father's" portrait, so he looks like a time traveller in his 1920s beige linen jacket, his natty yellow bow tie, and his boyish wig.

I come back to the rehearsal of the Gentleman Caller scene. "Well, I feel he's completely condescending," Karen declares flatly. "And I think *she's* a selfish *bitch!*" Jim fires back. It takes me a moment to realize they've reached the foolish stage. "I'm just getting silly," Jim laughs. "I can only be nice for so long, you know. I mean, girl, why don't you just get *lobotomized?*" Karen laughs now too. "How's business college?" Jim asks as Mr. O'Connor, back in character once more and with a yawn that makes Paul hoot in appreciation for the first time today, then stop them on a high note.

PAUL: The day before we shoot, we'll set it. Let's not dick around
   anymore.

JIM: I think I just talked myself into a cigarette.

He and Karen light up and Jim tells a long western joke. Paul tells one, too, in retaliation, and conversation dies. They sit in silence in the candlelight like war buddies at a campfire, with the battle about to begin and nothing left to say.

KAREN [*to Paul*]: What's *your* conception of this scene? I have no
   thread! Are we looking for a way these people would
   connect if it weren't for his having a girlfriend?

PAUL: It could never happen. They just loosen each other up. It's those flowers that unfold.

KAREN: You get to a point where if certain things haven't happened, they *can't* unfold!

PAUL: They will. The playwright's very deft. Even if you have discomfort, you almost can't make any mistakes. I know you think it's not working today, but it's been there and it'll be there again. I don't want to worry it to death. Once you're on the set, you'll both have different feelings. The main thing is, it's time for *me* to walk away from it. You know the props, the moves, the beats. You might want to work on it yourselves a couple of times, but that's up to you.

JIM: What's the schedule?

PAUL: Thursday night we film John going into the tenement. Friday we're on the set all day, rehearsing. Monday we start the picture.

KAREN: Maybe you're right. Maybe the set will help.

They fall silent again. Paul plays rat-a-tat-tat on his thighs with the palms of his hands, as if to say the discussion is over. Jim clears his throat. Karen walks to the buffet, where the chow mein is just arriving. Paul disappears to make a phone call. We undo our plastic containers of food in silence.

KAREN: It seems the more I do it, the more confused I get.

JIM: Having done it in the theatre all summer, we're *really* confused. I'm afraid when we get on the set we won't be able to do it at all—we'll want to come back here.

KAREN: For security.

We eat our chow mein. It's gluey and pale, like mucilage. Is that even a *word* anymore? Paul has returned to eat a token mouthful of it. Too concentrated on what lies ahead to notice that the rest of us still have chopsticks halfway to our lips, he announces, "Everyone onto the set!" and leads Karen and Jim, with Michael and Mary Bailey following, through workshops where the sets of other pictures are being built in blizzards of sawdust, then up those stinking stairs again to our stage. I wonder if Paul intends simply to give them another look at their future habitat, or whether he'll let them run the scene here to find the reassurance that has eluded them all morning.

People crawl over the set, magical union painters working under the keen-eyed stewardship of the master scenic artist of this film, Richard Ventre, who is responsible for executing a major part of Tony Walton's production design. All these artists, this Walton Brigade, turn down other assignments just to be available for the inspiration Tony's projects supply, and because he himself is never too busy to let them feel his recognition and support. Young women in yellow coveralls, on painting ladders, catch their first glimpse of Paul and appraise him coolly. I am riveted to their process of detailing: the metamorphosis, through superb technique, of paint and shellac and other mysterious substances into the mold and scabs of age. Riggers manhandle the fire escape on great iron chains that disappear into the grid above us. The hammering and sawing never stop.

As soon as they mount the steps up onto the set, Michael draws Paul aside into yet another discussion of the opening monologue, and Karen and Jim are forgotten. Paul notices them after a while and tells them they can go, and my curiosity about why he brought them up here is never satisfied. Jim lumbers over, looking as though he could use someone to talk to.

JIM: Whenever I look up I see you writing. Sometimes it looks as if you're writing down everything we say. Other times you seem to be writing things you're only seeing inside your head. What are you doing?

STEWART: Both. Trying to document this process. Being a snoop.

He seems to want to talk about Paul. He tells me how eagerly he had looked forward to working with him to learn "what film acting was really all about," and how shocked he was when Paul told him, "After thirty-five years of trying, I'm just beginning to learn." I suspect that this morning has made Jim realize that the guru he's looking for had better be himself, for he's finding it hard to understand what Paul is saying or how he sees the goals of the scene: "It's sometimes like pulling teeth to get it out of him," Jim confides, and he feels adrift, unmoored from purpose, playing separate moments separately in the hope that something will make them coalesce. The suggestions Paul offers occasionally seem too cryptic to understand, he says, and sometimes when Paul suggests a "piece of behavior," he omits the reasons beneath it. Telling me all this, Jim seems particularly vulnerable, and I appreciate the trust he's offering: he must be aware that, for better or worse, I could choose to be a conduit to Paul. Many months after this encounter, he'll be able to say, looking back on this morning:

JIM: It was a very frustrating morning. I wanted to be anyplace but there. It was one of those awkward rehearsals where you don't understand what someone's trying to get you to do, or where you're being asked to go, or what it is you're trying to achieve. You feel you're not any good as an actor, and what's dangerous about that is that in becoming frightened, you become angry, and then you begin to turn off, turn off the process, turn off the people around you.

Here we were, sitting down, going through this scene move by move, and all the focus was on the pillow, the gum, the things that seemed to me incidental, a three-hour exercise in bits, arbitrary behavior, externals. In Tennessee Williams, if you don't get the first building block right, everything after it is wrong, and you can't say, "Well, we'll come back to it." If it feels phony, it never *stops* feeling phony, and there's nothing more excruciating than to have to do it anyway.

I didn't even want to rehearse that afternoon, but I'm glad I did because we got to a point where I began to *become* those externals that Paul was giving me. They began to give me a kind of physical behavior that let me *feel* where I was going, let me realize with my body that I was someone consumed with self, with cutting a figure, with how I looked. Paul was working from the outside in with me, as opposed to the inside out, and he wanted me to show him what O'Connor's problem was, what was missing in him, why his dreams were never fulfilled: he may not admit consciously that life isn't going to be sweet to him, but deep in his gut he knows it, and has known it from the start. And Paul wanted me to put that into behavior. I remember thinking, all through that incredibly frustrating morning, "If this goes on any longer he's going to jump up and say, 'Get out of the way, kid, here's the way to do it!'" But he was always positive and patient, always open, uncomplicated, generous.

But those realizations would come later. Now Jim says that he was temporarily relieved last night when Paul covered the mouthpiece of the phone he was speaking on to say, "Nice work," to him. I ask whether he knew what that referred to, but his face empties. He says he thinks so, but it's hard to hold on to, and I can't tell him, without breaking confidentiality, what Paul has told me about Jim's natural connections with the character that make it impossible to choose wrong, whatever choice he makes. I think Jim wants "loose time" with Paul, natural time, away from rehearsal, where he can be himself with him and establish contact in a personal way that has nothing to do with the picture, where they can just be two guys together. But finding loose time with Paul is like finding Atlantis.

JIM: The obstacle Paul and I have to come to grips with is our communication. He doesn't spend a lot of time talking about things, and constantly leaves out antecedents so I'm never quite sure what he's saying—and never having worked with him, or known him before, we don't have any shorthand to fall back on. And we have the added inconvenience of his being Paul Newman. For thirty years he's had to deal with people trying to get a look at his eyes, so I think he covers quite a bit, and one tends—I guess—to defer to him. On the other hand, we want to pick his brain, that's what he's there for, and I'm hoping I can find some way to communicate. I really think he wants to be accessible.

Jim seems so open to any comment I might have about his performance that I'm afraid to tell him anything, so I shift the conversation to reinforce his original sense of Paul. When Paul and I have worked together before, I tell him, I participated with my blood, not just my eyes and ears as I'm having to do now, because it was always my script he was doing. And I'd be mystified by some of his directions, confused by some of his choices, enraged by some of the cuts he asked me to make, hurt by the distance he might suddenly put between us, and could see much less clearly then, appreciate much less when I was in the thick of it, how much he was supporting me, how graceful he was with the actors and how he respected them, how determined he was never to interfere with their process or with mine, how reticent he was to push except when he needed to, and how reluctant he was, ever, to frustrate a creative impulse, or to demand, by an overlord's attitude, an overlord's due.

We stand here speaking for a long time together, looking up at our composite portrait of Paul and trying busily to retouch whatever blemishes our discussion might have put there. But from what I have seen today, I think I'm right in believing that they and the scene will be rudderless until Paul does a lot more subtextual digging, and finds them a fresher wind to sail with and a clearer course to follow.

Tenth
Day of
Rehearsal

I am greeted by Burtt Harris, who tells me about the trip last
night to see the East Harlem relic that will double as Amanda's
St. Louis apartment house in the only exterior shot in the picture
to be filmed at an actual location. Paul stood in for John
Malkovich in order to time Tom's walk from the boarded-up
tenement door, around through the alley, to the fire escape
where he makes his decision to climb to that long-ago apartment.

Joanne hurries in, dispensing good-mornings like doughnuts. When she gets to me, I open up the ratty old fridge to
show her the tapioca I made last night as a treat for Paul, who is
as addicted to this unpredictable pudding as he is to chocolate-
covered grapefruit rinds. I had been too engrossed in the TV
movie I was watching to keep track of the number of table-
spoons of extra-large pearl tapioca that I was pouring into the
milk, so I just kept throwing in more. The chilled casserole

practically bounces with elasticity, but Joanne emits that special cooing sound that the sight of a pudding produces in her; when she ventures to touch it, it hurls her back like a rubber ball: it will have none of her.

Paul arrives with music on his mind, takes Burtt aside to tell him that he wants to invite Henry Mancini to compose the score. He doesn't want an orchestra, he says, just an oboe, a cello, and a bassoon. He turns on a recording of Paul Bowles's lovely incidental music, composed for the original Broadway production of the play, and Joanne and John rehearse to it, allowing themselves to be washed by its mood, like dancers. We are transported to a time when, within these same studio walls, other actors, stars of a silent screen, acted to the music of violins. Joanne sighs when the music ends. "Lovely," she says. "So curiously right. It was never a case of Tennessee just bringing in a composer; he was bringing in a friend, who could compose." I ask Paul whether he plans to have Henry Mancini replace the Paul Bowles score, but he assures me that he wants the Bowles themes to remain. Mancini's task will be to implement them with original themes of his own and also to create, based on old recordings Paul has been receiving from a friendly disc jockey in St. Louis, the sad blue wail of Depression-era jazz as it might have been performed by the Paradise Dance Hall's band across the way.

This was to be another walk-through rehearsal, just for positions, with Mary Bailey reading Amanda's lines again so Joanne can save her voice, but Joanne's throat is fine today and she will speak for herself from now on. Mary surrenders with pretended grace and the forced smile of a lady-in-waiting who's been whacked in the face by a fish head. Will she *never* get to play this role? I send her a friendly wink of consolation that means "Tear up your Equity card," and I have to put ice packs on the look she sends me back.

They are rehearsing the Annunciation scene. Joanne is all sprightly expectation as John teases her about the gentleman caller from his perch above on the ladder that is standing in for the fire escape. She hops with delight, clapping her hands and skipping after him as he drags his sensuality across the living room like a slave's dayload of cotton. The more excited she gets, the more he slumps under the weight of it, until his whole bone-less body slithers onto its chair and implodes with exhaustion.

PAUL: How are these positions for you?

MICHAEL: Terrible, of course—what do you think?

JOHN: Well, I don't care where I sit as long as I can have bad posture.

Paul moves him from rocker to couch just to make Michael happy, and receives a little bow of acknowledgment.

PAUL: Joanne. Bring a footstool next time. One of the ones your father made.

JOANNE: Where are those things? He made three. The girls keep borrowing them to take to college, then they all change schools and leave them there.

This time John does a slow-motion dive onto the couch, like a Slinky toy tumbling off a step.

PAUL: Oh, I like the way that looks, nifty and snaky! Let's shoot it in CinemaScope, Michael. That's the only ratio wide enough for snakes.

Along with the rest of the hair that John has surrendered to the Merchant Marine, his little blond punker's pigtail has finally gone. In the lull, while we wait for Karen and Jim to arrive from their dressing rooms, Joanne pulls Paul close to her chair and presses her face against him, arms around his waist. She is always the one who reaches, to pick off a thread, to straighten his hair, to hold his head, and whatever she does, he goes limp with submission, as helpless as a dog having its belly scratched.

JOANNE: I'm worried about the beer.

PAUL: What beer?

JOANNE: In the Gentleman Caller scene. Amanda would never permit beer in the house.

PAUL: I told them not to bring it in.

JOANNE: There wouldn't even be any in the refrigerator! That was a *northern* thing to do. Only Yankees drank beer. "Yankees and niggras and po' people!" That's why the dandelion wine's so special, why she presents it the way she does. She'd serve lemonade—or ice water with lots of ice—and never cubes, big chunks!

PAUL: I'll lose this one gracefully.

Now Joe Caracciolo, the handsome young associate producer, comes in with some new candle mock-ups. Tony Walton had been as worried as I when he saw the screen tests of the candles: the shadows of their aluminum cores that concealed the bulbs in the tapers could be clearly seen through the glowing wax the moment the wicks were lighted, and Joe had volunteered to find an alternative. What he has come up with is a practical and ingenious invention of his own, but while it eliminates the shadow problem, it also eliminates the lovely glow of wax, so

Michael votes for the original and Paul agrees. Joe's dedication impresses me: not only the cleanness of his presentation to Paul, or his courtesy without obsequiousness, but also the fact that he is beginning to show what is already so seasoned in Burtt—the ability to anticipate the needs of others, to offer options without pressing his cause, and to protect the members of the harried creative team by taking on burdens that there is simply no time for them to carry under the pressures of rehearsal and production. He leaves, taking his prototype with him, showing no injury that his idea hasn't been used.

Time passes. Other details are attended to, and I can begin to sense that restlessness that always marks the end of any phase in the making of a movie. Drew goes upstairs to see what is keeping Jim and Karen. Joanne massages Paul's shoulders, trying to detach her mind from what he's begun to discuss with Michael, the monologues again: since all the monologues of the play are spoken from the present, must John always be costumed and made up as Tom-of-the-present every time he speaks one? Or having once taken us into the past at the beginning, can he remain in appearance as he was in the past even though he is meant, during the monologues, to be speaking from the present? Michael appears absolutely fixed in his determination that, despite the obvious contradictions, once in the past Tom should speak all his monologues from the past until the drama is done, and we should not see him again in his present-day makeup or costume, nor see the apartment as the ruin it is today, until he has exorcised Laura and come back to the present at the end. Paul is "not comfortable at all" with that idea: he wants Tom to return to the present for all of his monologues, to have a three-day growth of beard when he is in the present, and be clean-shaven whenever he is in the past. Joanne walks away, leaving the field to the men. Michael says it will "destroy the flow" if, visually, we keep coming back to the present every time there's a monologue. They should seem no more than passing comments; once inside memory, we should *stay* inside memory! The men plant their opposing statements like battle flags and stand there breathing at each other. Michael's proposal troubles me: to keep Tom in the past for all those monologues would make him seem to have understood what he could not have understood at the time. In order to exorcise the past he must be able to watch his young self *struggle* in the past, witness his own part in the *creation* of that past, but from his present, more experienced, point of view.

The argument goes on all over the room, with Paul in strategic withdrawal and Michael in relentless pursuit. He even comes to stand over Paul while he's trying to eat his sandwich, then drags him over to the model and demands that he decide at least what the scenery should be behind the monologues, regardless of Tom's costume or the state or length of his beard. Does Paul want the furnished past, or the derelict present? He must decide.

PAUL: A fire escape is a fire escape.

MICHAEL: No! One is the past, one is the present. Something has happened to it: it is different!

Paul chews his lip.

MICHAEL: So what will you do?

Paul rolls his eyes wide and turns an idiot stare on him. Slack-jawed and with a sudden cleft-palate nasality, he clowns: "I dunno!" and lurches away like a yeti to find his sandwich. Michael sighs, knowing that nothing is settled, and drains the scalding drink someone hands him as though it were cool spring water.

Jim Naughton and Karen arrive in a breezy mood, and John, whose spirit seems to have lightened as the darkness around him increased, is gregarious and frisky. Joanne joins them at the table for the supper segment of the Gentleman Caller scene, glad to have something to do. Paul steals up on Jim from behind and slaps a knife and fork into his fists so they stick straight up like prisoner utensils. Jim likes it and it makes Joanne laugh. I can see that she's on the verge of breaking up and is trying very hard not to, but John provokes it:

JOANNE [*as Amanda*]: "Tom, would you like to say grace?"

JOHN [*only more or less as Tom*]: No! I'm busy eating!

Joanne stares at him. He picks up a curl of sawdust from the floor and lays it on her plate. She starts laughing inside, but her mouth remains firm.

JOHN: Why, what are you eating, Mother?

PAUL: Okay, that's enough.

JOHN [*with an angel's smile*]: Don't you want to see the rest?

PAUL: I'm not sure I can handle it.

JOHN: I think we should have different things on our plates, don't you? Laura should have Librium. I should have amphetamines. I don't know *what* we should give the gentleman caller!

JIM: I think I should get out of here!

Joanne's laughter explodes all over the table. Everything sounds funny to her now, and Tennessee's text, in those infrequent moments when they get back to it, sounds funniest of all.

John clears the table endlessly while everyone waits, slamming down again and again the same silverware on the same four plates as he stacks them over and over. I think of Beatrice Lillie before her entrance as the chambermaid in a sketch, the sound of her ridiculous orthopedic shoes stamping up and down in the wings for what seemed like five minutes before she finally opened the door and said to the dowager who employed her, "You rang, ma'am? Well, *stop!*" Things pass beyond hope when John marches into the "kitchen" and throws all the props on the floor. The great Joanne Woodward has simply gone bye-bye and turned into Billie Burke before our eyes. Paul watches tolerantly, knowing that this is just another spasm in the process and, like the hiccups, is bound to pass away.

They settle down and run through to the end of the play. Sitting alone and no longer smiling, Michael despairs over all the unanswered questions. John goes to him inquiringly during a break and I see worried words exchanged. We have reached Amanda's heartbroken rejection of Tom just prior to the final fade-out: "Go to the moon, you selfish dreamer!" and Tom's plaintive exorcism of his sister's memory: "Oh, Laura, Laura, I tried to leave you behind me, but I am more faithful than I intended to be! I reach for a cigarette, I cross the street, I run into a movie or a bar, I buy a drink, I speak to the nearest stranger—anything that can blow your candles out!—For nowadays the world is lit by lightning! Blow out your candles, Laura—and so—goodbye!" The voices are hardly stilled before John breaks the mood and announces that he wants to make his final exit down the fire escape.

JOHN: Tom says, "I descended the steps of this fire escape for the last time." I don't think that means he left that night, after the bitch-fight over the gentleman caller. I think he hung around, he wrote poems, he got fired, he gradually turned into his father, and then he sneaked away when Laura wasn't home. Down the fire escape—because that's his shitty, secret way, the same way he always sneaked home when he got drunk and found some fifteen-year-old boy to have sex with.

MICHAEL: To me, he doesn't go anywhere, only back into the present. As soon as his mother says, "Go to the moon, you selfish dreamer," then he is back in the circular dolly doing his final monologue, and Laura is sliding around him in a bigger circle, and when he says, "Blow out your candles, Laura," we see her doing that, and finally she just disappears, and he is free from that memory for always.

Paul seems to sense the walls moving in on him. He rises suddenly, grips John and Michael by their elbows, and steers them rather forcefully into the anteroom. I take my metal chair to the door where I can eavesdrop.

PAUL: There are lots of ways to do this, guys, but when he starts that final monologue, "I didn't go to the moon, I went much further," there aren't going to be any fire escapes! You see Amanda comforting Laura, or Laura comforting her, whoever has the serenity to comfort whom, then they've got to disappear and we're left on Tom's face. The people of the past are gone, vanished. He's back in the present, in the arch of what used to be the living room, and maybe you think you see their shadows on the wall, maybe you think you see a shadow blotting out some glow of candles on a wall that's really in the present, but, Michael, I don't see how you can think of sliding the literal image of Laura into the present again once the past is behind us and we're on his face, because that's where the emotion is, fellas, and that's where the picture has to end.

Nobody speaks for some time. Then Michael brings up a tangential idea—to use the long hall that bisects the apartment as a kind of time tunnel, an avenue between past and present: the camera would travel back along it from the *tableau vivant* of Amanda and Laura comforting each other in the candlelight, back, back, back past an actor who, for this one shot, would double as Tom-of-the-Past, and discover John behind him, dressed as Tom-of-Today, watching the memory fade from where he stands at the far end of the hall. Boxes within boxes. On "I didn't go to the moon, I went much further" he would lead us forward again down the hall, through the arch, into the living area, and we would find it partially restored to the derelict present. "And as he enters the circle where the camera is revolving," Michael dreams for one last time, "Laura will appear fleetingly, and circle around him until he says, 'Blow out your candles,' and then she is finally exorcised and every vestige of the past will disappear." "Lots of ways to do it," Paul repeats, weary of the argument, but John has heard Michael's petition about keeping Tom in the past for all his monologues and agrees with him passionately that to alter his appearance every time he recites one would take the heat out of the story by damming its flow.

JOHN: You know what it does if you keep him dressed for the past, Paul? It makes him more of a magician! He can be in the past and the present simultaneously that way. It's "softer" than going back and forth.

PAUL: It's very disturbing for me to have the logic of the middle different from the beginning-and-end logic just because it's convenient for us.

JOHN: Doesn't your way raise questions of logic too? Like how can Tom remember the Gentleman Caller scene when he wasn't in the room when it happened?

PAUL: At one point I thought of putting him there, but an observer would be an intrusion.

JOHN: So you simply assume he can be in two places at once. If you do what Michael suggests, you'll be able to have him in the past and the present at the same time too. You get both sides of him. In the house—and in the past—he's a spoiled little shit-ass who won't comb his hair, but the minute he steps onto the fire escape, even if it looks like the fire escape of the past and he's dressed for the past, you get the whole other side of him, the present side, looking back. Both aspects, bam, bam! Simultaneously.

PAUL: And what about the audience? Are they going to sit forward on the edge of their seats going, "Aha! I got it!"? Or will they just be sitting back going, "Huh?"

No one can answer. When we are heading for the car that will take us home, Burtt reminds Paul that he has left his bag behind, and Paul runs back to retrieve it.

PAUL: Someday someone's going to say, "Paul, where's your ass? You lost your ass!" And I won't even be surprised. I will probably have left it in a cab.

As we drive through the mid-Manhattan traffic to the lab where the most recent makeup tests will be screened, nobody says a word. Paul has pulled into himself so far that his jacket seems sizes too large. He gazes out of one window, Michael the other. They see nothing of the scenery, only the shrinking time between now and Monday when the picture will begin, only all those decisions that remain unmade, like beds from which sleepers have fled.

Images appear on the screen. There's too much contrast between their skin tones when John puts his face beside Karen's. Michael suggests that they lighten her a little.

PAUL: Won't that make her look chalky? Of course if it does we can always change her name: "Hey, Chalky!"

STEWART: "Blow out your candles, Chalky."

The laughter doesn't help. In the silence we can hear each other's nerves.

Eleventh
Day of
Rehearsal

Paul enters jauntily, a country boy kicking his way down a lane, suspenders over his blue farm shirt. I show him his college grades, which I have secured from his alma mater, Kenyon, in connection with some research I have been doing, but he studies them coldly and doesn't react. Until I saw his entrance application on top of the pile, I had no idea that he once attended the University of Pennsylvania as well, and he had forgotten it entirely:

PAUL: My God, I don't remember anything about it except for smuggling a case of beer over a wall! I was a great smuggler. I smuggled another one into the Case Hotel in Mount Vernon, Ohio. Threw a blanket over it and carried it in. The guy at the desk said, "What you got there?" I said, "A dead student."

The rehearsal hall seems depopulated somehow. Mary is here, and Michael. John and Jim are over there, getting their coffee. Karen knits. I talk with her awhile. She says she's been worrying through the nights: all the good ideas that come to her in the dark seem terrible by morning; and do I know that Amanda, Laura, and Tom come from an earlier work of Tennessee's, a short story called "Portrait of a Woman in Glass"? I realize now why the room seems empty: Joanne's not here.

PAUL: Should we all just walk around and wait for something to happen?

Now she hurries in, sporting her new Amanda haircut and full of apologies for being late. Without preamble, Paul starts the rehearsal, the last that will be held in this room; they must be finished here by four to shoot at the Harlem location. Joanne is gay and quick and light in her opening scene, struggling to maintain the pleasant appearance of normalcy in this dark, obsessive home, animated by a hope so long pretended that she's made it real, and I see again what Paul meant when he said that hers was the only Amanda whose gentlemen callers actually seemed to have called. But as her soliloquy ends and she spies her wayward husband's picture on the wall, her contempt for him is so strong that it makes her shrewish. I see Paul give Mary a note.

PAUL: John! The moves you made in the monologue I may ask you to repeat when we shoot. Your instinct is right. Joanne, don't flutter when you touch him at the table. Don't pet. And when you're talking about gentlemen callers, just brush up against those memories, brush up and let them go, don't dwell.

JOANNE: I was only trying to entertain my children with them.

PAUL: Well, brush them away as they come. Brush each troubled thought or marvelous thought away, so you can go on to the next. This was Rachel: [*He pinches his lips together till they're white.*] And this is Amanda: [*He pretends to brush a fly away from his face.*] That's my signal—no more "Pinch it!" And when you look at your husband's picture at the end, and you say, "I could have been Mrs. Duncan J. Fitzhugh, but what did I do? I just went out of my way and picked your father!" it's much too strong!

But Joanne insists she be allowed to have "one awful moment of naked resentment, then do what we always do in families: take it back." She wants Paul to allow her that moment, but he thinks it could destroy her fragility as an addict of memory and a weaver of illusion.

PAUL: John, I like you being behind Laura with your hands on her shoulders. I like the contact, being physically in league against Amanda. What do you think? Too much incest again?

JOHN and KAREN: No!

Paul notices Michael in a corner, incubating the eggs of worry, and interrupts his rehearsal to go to him. "I made a decision last night," Paul says: whenever John is doing a monologue, he will be unshaven; he will wear the costume and makeup of the present and be seen in the wreckage of the present-day apartment. He will not remain in the past to do the monologues. The glove is down. Michael picks it up: once Tom steps into the past at the start, he argues, he must remain there for all his monologues, be seen inside its scenery, be clad in its costumes, and only "be of the present" in his point of view. John comes over and takes Michael's side: the only way Tom can hold on to his memories and relive them is to play by the rules of memory and stay inside their world until the end. Paul looks from John to Michael.

PAUL: The reason I want Tom to keep coming back to the present is to remind us what it cost him to run away from the past. He has paid a terrible price. He's haunted. He has failed. He's probably a drunkard now. He hasn't been able to live one moment of life past the moment when he abandoned them. I want to see all that, every time he talks to us. That's part of the story too, and that's why he must keep coming back into the present.

He leaves them and returns to his rehearsal to run the Deception scene. I can still hear them talking in the corner, and so can he. When it's time for the Quarrel scene, he goes to fetch John.

PAUL: Let's just walk through the next passage, just wander through the lines.

JOHN: What I'd like to wander through is the emotions.

But he doesn't. Joanne has been told to save her voice and she feels terrible about it, but John plays it self-protectively too, with none of his divine Nijinsky madness that he brought to it before. Its absence troubles Paul. John should let the images carry him high, he says; he must grow hot with them if he is to reach that curtain line that allows no possible retreat: "You ugly, babbling old witch!"

David Ray, the young British-born wizard of film editing, has wandered in to observe these proceedings, and keeps getting up to restock himself with carrots, like a chipmunk trying to beat the snow. His sneakered foot keeps time with his chewing. He is inscrutable. Michael, calmer now, comes over with a peace offering for Paul:

MICHAEL: Do you think maybe it would be nice with the "Opium dens" speech if John would be cavorting up and down on the fire escape instead of being again stuck in the room?

Even the mention of "fire escape" makes John smile as though he'd just swallowed a Fabergé egg and smuggled it out of the Hermitage Museum, but he says nothing. Paul's smile is a little different:

PAUL: Michael, it's really interesting how things that bother you don't bother me, and things that bother me don't bother you. You have trouble going from the past to the present for John's monologues, and to me, if there's a door to come in, that's the door you come in—unless you're so drunk you have to sneak up a fire escape. It's really fascinating.

JOANNE: Can we stop this . . . philosophical discussion? *I* don't need to know how he comes in, any more than I knew my children used the windows and the roof. They'd hang by their nails from the drainpipes and drop to the lawn. I don't know why I never found a pile of bodies!

At lunch I go up to see how the "dressing of the set" is progressing, and encounter Jim Naughton there, alone. He asks what I meant the other day when I said certain things about his performance seemed "so clear to me." Apparently he wants me to tell him what did not, but I can't even recall that part of our conversation. The fact that Paul may still want to cut out Tom's monologue about Mr. O'Connor worries him greatly because it's the only place where the gentleman caller is described, the only chance the audience has to understand that the flaw he carries today has been with him since high school: desperate feelings of inadequacy under a determined self-delusion. Jim says it's nearly impossible to play both dimensions simultaneously, the bravado he presents to Laura, which she never penetrates and which is therefore not revealed for what it is, and also the uncertainty hiding under it. Some of his history and behavior can be observed only by Tom, whose speech also provides, if not insight, speculation: the question of why Mr. O'Connor should have chosen to befriend Tom Wingfield, out of all the other workers at the warehouse—an unhappy, reclusive, alcoholic closet gay who writes poems in the john—is not raised anywhere else. I urge Jim to appeal directly to Paul, to set diffidence aside and insist on time with him before being called back weeks from now to shoot. We descend to the rehearsal stage together, but before Jim can collar him, Paul vanishes into conference with Michael again. Jim rolls his eyes at me, shrugs, accepts his rehearsal call for Friday, and goes. Paul calls to me from the anteroom to ask what I'm sitting here writing, and I cover these notes rather guiltily. If Isherwood was a camera, I am a notebook.

In a few minutes we have to leave for Harlem, but they continue to sit in the anteroom, talking and talking. The assistant cameraman and David Ray have joined them. Michael never changes his tone of voice or drops his smile, never shows impatience with Paul or makes him feel wrong, or rigid, or too timid to dare, never becomes exasperated with him for frustrating parts of his cinematic dream.

PAUL: Yes, I can hear voices that shake me out of the present, and yes, I can see fragments that persist and that pull me into the past, but I don't go all the way with you, Michael, because my mind moves very readily back and forth through time. It's not based on a question of makeup, or costume, or scenery, and I'm puzzled by your concern even while I'm respectful of your logic. But I think, "Jesus Christ! Am I that far off base?"

MICHAEL: He announces, "I'm taking you back into the past." He *announces* it! "Let's see what happens there! Come with me! Take my hand! I take you back to see what happened there!" That means once we are in the story, we have to stay in the story, visually, until the end, until it's over!

PAUL: Why? If he's a magician of time, why can't he keep violating time? Why can't he leave it whenever he needs to, to talk to us? I don't see the problem, fellas!

MICHAEL: I'm desperate now.

DAVID RAY: I think we should agree on a philosophy and then determine the specifics of it—

MICHAEL: Just tell me where to put the camera! Tell me what lens to use and I will shoot it!

Paul is tight and silent, looking at Michael. Michael rises and hurries out.

MICHAEL: I'll see you on location in an hour.

The rest go too, leaving Paul by himself. He continues to sit there ruminating for several minutes. "We've had a contretemps," he says to himself in disbelief. "Michael and I have had a contretemps." And he's afraid that Michael might leave the picture. I go with him to Joanne's dressing room, where he tells her all about it; he shares it with his assistant, Marcia Franklin, on the phone; he confides it to Tony Walton when he passes him in the hall. *"Contretemps:* an inopportune occurrence,"* says my dictionary, a nice definition a weekend away from production. But I can hear Paul saying the same of World War III. In a rain of rock and fire that's just the way he'd put it, "We seem to be having an inopportune occurrence."

The limousine carries us smoothly toward his apartment where he can snatch an hour of sleep before the shoot. During the drive he says, "I don't want a frustrated and disappointed Michael who only does my will under duress. I want his creative best." But he doesn't want it at the cost of the vision he thinks is right. Yet *is* it right? he asks himself. Could *he* be the one who's being willful? And having offered Michael so much creative freedom in their partnership, has he the right to withdraw it now?

He asks my views about the "contretemps." I say I can accept either plan since both offer clear conceptual lines to me. I can certainly believe, along with Michael, that Tom could comment on his own experience from deep within his visualization of the past without ever disturbing his younger physical appearance or the details of the home he has invoked with such an effort of his poetic imagination. This "time travel" could be helped even more, I suggest, by having Tom grow physically younger during his first monologue, so that by the time he reaches the end of it, he, like the place he is describing, has entirely regressed. By completing the monologue after the physical changes in him have been accomplished, he would have established his ability to speak to us from the past while belonging both to the past and to the present, to immerse himself in the experience he lived through and at the same time to stand apart from it. Paul seems drawn to this idea while we are still in the limousine, but by the time we arrive upstairs it seems either to have lost its appeal or to have been forgotten. We never speak of it again.

He paces the flowered carpet of the living room, agitated in a way I've seldom seen him, his shirt dark blue with sweat. He pauses to chew at his lip, stare down at the reservoir below. He seems unsteady and unsure. The chill awareness that he's starting without a concept only adds to the discomfort he always feels in opposing anyone he likes, and the tendency to mistrust his own opinion only grows when to trust it brings unhappiness and conflict. He takes a call from someone on his racing team, gnaws one bite out of a wedge of Israeli melon, puts on a CD of classical guitar and turns it off, paces again. I watch him for several minutes wondering how I can serve him as a friend, then suggest that the issue might go deeper than the question it seems to ask, right down to the difference between two artists, Paul and Michael, between the blue- and the brown-eyed people, between the real and the surreal, the conscious and the unconscious, the waking state and the dream state. He sits on the couch. I ask him to tell me again his original vision of the opening sequence, the way he told it on his stone porch in Connecticut, way back at the beginning of last summer. He looks surprised, but he gets to his feet again and starts to describe a series of images so unaffected and clear that I'm touched all over again. I can see how, in his desire to graft himself to another person's vision, in the ping-pong escalation of circular dollies and sliding wagons bearing living statues of the past, he has watered his own conception with doubt and nearly disenfranchised what he believes in.

PAUL: He comes up the fire escape, steps in, and creates his own close-up. Then his point of view: this is the front of the room, right? Here's the fire escape over here.

STEWART: I'm in the room, you're on the fire escape?

PAUL: You're in the hall, almost. Then the camera comes around this way, around this deserted place, this derelict apartment, right? Derelict, derelict, derelict as he looks around at every corner of it and the camera takes his point of view—out the window, at the fireplace, up the hallway, back this way—and right here he snaps on the match.

STEWART: You mean his hand comes into the shot?

PAUL: The camera comes by his hand. It lights a kitchen match. Then a cigarette. He says: "Tricks in my pocket . . . things up my sleeve. . . . I take you back to an alley in St. Louis. . . ." We follow him—we start to hear music from the Paradise Dance Hall, just a little sense of it over there—

STEWART: Where's the camera now?

PAUL: On his back—

STEWART: And he's looking out the window?

PAUL: Out to the fire escape. "In Spain there was revolution . . . The play is memory. . . ." The camera's off his face now— on an object up here, out of focus—but the light comes through it. And at that point, we wipe. It becomes two separate shots joined by an invisible wipe. Now the light becomes an object that *turns* in the light, a little glass animal held in a hand. We see Laura. Camera comes around this way to Joanne pacing with a phone in her hand—around the apartment now a second time—but this time it's not derelict—we're in the past—her African violets—the picture of the father on this wall, and then the camera comes down like this, and John's leaning up against the archway, still costumed for the present, and in back of him is the derelict apartment. So the front room in this second shot is furnished as the past, but the back hall is the derelict apartment of the present. And when he says, "He left us a long time ago," I'll flood the hall behind him with light, build up the light till it burns him out: "Hello, goodbye!" and he's gone—

He grows more and more excited as he talks, more and more confident as he hears himself recite his own idea. A few minutes later he's throwing water on his face. "I think I'm going to ask Michael to implement my vision," he says. "I believe in it." The cold sun stands just above the Palisades. Michael's "magic hour" is nearly here. We go downstairs and are driven to the location.

A crowd of silent black neighborhood people waits behind police barricades to watch the preparations for the shoot. The street has been wetted down and laced with cables. In the fading light, reflectors wobble booster highlights onto the house. Dolly tracks running diagonally from curb to curb leave only a bus-wide lane for the downtown traffic. Half a dozen Hispanic policemen keep watchful eyes on the crowd but these people are extremely polite, and even when Paul steps out of his limousine there is very little pointing and excitement. John Malkovich appears in his Merchant Marine jacket. I'm disappointed to see that he has decided to wear a hairpiece, not only for the past— as planned—but for the present as well, and to learn that Paul agreed to it in "the interest of actor's comfort."

Paul squints at the light and frets. It's a flat, dull gray, and getting flatter. The old building rises from its pillars looking as lonely on its rubble-strewn lot as a painting by Edward Hopper. Grips and cableboys herd the great giraffe of a crane onto its starting mark. Its remote camera, controlled by little wheels on a television monitor a hundred feet away, will allow all key personnel to share from the ground the view the camera receives at the top of its boom. Our little rehearsal cadre of the last eleven days is nearly swallowed up in the expanded crew that will surround it from now on: there will be dozens of new faces, and dozens of new names that have to go with them. Paul seems to have withdrawn again, worried, I suppose, about the assertiveness he may have to demonstrate in declaring the supremacy of his own idea to Michael. They have scarcely spoken at all since we came out here.

Shot follows shot as the twilight deepens, and objects appear brighter on the monitor screen than they are in life. John Malkovich has disappeared entirely into Tom Wingfield and will not come out again until the filming ends. It is Tom who now leads the camera forward, climbs the steps to the tenement door and peers in through the glass, trots down and walks through the alley, pausing once to make certain we are with him, then starts up the fire escape on his way into the past. He must repeat it again and again, his face smudged mother-of-pearl over the turned-up collar of his pea coat, his eyes the frightened eyes of a man we have never seen till now. The complexity of the look he gives the camera, so defensive even as it appeals, moves me deeply and I sense this performance will be wonderful. Although what he has to do this evening is simple and small, committing himself to film makes it significant, for this fragment of the character represents a decision, his secret's out.

Marcia Franklin, Paul's assistant, has discovered where the cookies are and leads me to them; we move like two conspirators through the gloaming. As darkness envelops us, the shots come faster and faster. I take a last look at the activity around me as it fades like the final frame of a film. There will be a last, touch-up rehearsal tomorrow and then the process I've been chronicling will be over. My final glimpse of Tom Wingfield shows me only his unguarded sweetness. Paul and Michael stand side by side, touching but not talking, ready to squeeze one last shot out of this vanished day. I reach for a handkerchief and am happy to find a cookie in my pocket that I didn't know was there. It's got a candied cherry on it I can suck on all the way downtown.

Final
Day of
Rehearsal

They have moved to the shooting stage upstairs. Familiar old Stage I, our dungeon, is empty now. They have taken away the phones and a janitor is wheeling a bin through the place, peeling marking tape off the floor. It's like coming into a room where someone has died.

I go up to Stage H. The buffet table has followed them upstairs like a guilty conscience, and doubled in length because now there's a crew to feed. The Irish soda breads are piled like cannonballs at the corners of a village green. I'm stunned by the conviction of the set now. The predominant colors, like those of Roman walls, are sienna, umber, and ocher, grayed by the mournful "daylight" seeping in through the window shades and the feeble wattage of old lamps. The gels in the hot lights smell sweet.

Richard Ventre, who's been supervising all the young men

and women painting sadness on the walls, introduces me to Richard Prouse, former scenic designer for the Albuquerque Light Opera and all the other theatres in that town. A tall, gentle young man, he speaks of his admiration for Tony Walton's artistry, and of Tony's appreciation for this handpicked band of "scenics" who, crouching in every corner, reaching high from ladders along the walls, paint and sand and burnish away in silence, proudly expecting no thanks and leaving no signature. Richard seems pleased when I tell him that, to me, the set is "writing," that it speaks as eloquently as Tennessee did of the valor of Amanda. Its tiny conservatory, where her plants are starved for light, is the visual history of her dogged survival, and her care of the bric-a-brac and the weary furniture is her statement that a regard for charm can be a rock in the foundation of the curious courage that lets this family live. What Richard and his colleagues have created here with their detailing is no easy coffin to escape from.

He tells me that scenics are seldom recognized, or noticed. They contrive the habitats others will occupy and, when they are done, depart in the night without ever encountering the actors or director they provide for; these arrive with the sun like a gang of hunters finding a hut in the woods. Richard tells me that on certain other shoots the scenics aren't even invited to help themselves from the buffet. Paul has passed through here a number of times during the past several days, he says, but has spoken to no one, so everybody's still wondering whether he likes their set. He forgets sometimes that people need acknowledgment: perhaps because he has never been convinced by the compliments he receives, he finds them unimportant to give. But once in a while he fairly drips with praise: months from now, after the picture is finished, Jim Naughton will receive a gift from Paul, a bottle of wine with a card Jim treasures: "Saw the rough cut today. Newman."

I'm leaning on a section of the fire escape as I finish my talk with Richard. A carpenter named Lou comes up and gently moves me away: this rusty "iron" I'm leaning on is wood.

Joanne, John, Karen, and Paul arrive below and climb to the set. Only Joanne speaks to the scenics. She goes from room to room enraptured, touching the wainscoting here, bamboo side tables there. She wants to take everything home, even the stove whose iron feet have worn through the linoleum to the artfully painted illusion of grimy wood beneath. Karen, smoke pouring into her eyes from her cigarette, kneels before the glass menagerie as if it were a shrine and makes friends with all her animals. The set is called to order like a court, and Paul, surrounded by the full complement of his crew for the first time, begins running the action for positions and camera moves. He's in a silly mood, beginning to feel a tickle of that precious fear that fuels him. "Okay, let's shoot it!" he cries. "Wake me at noon!" He mutters that his whole conception about memory has fallen apart now that he's seen the set. I ask what he means, but he walks away with his mind on something else.

There is too little space, there are too many people. As the actors run through the scenes, testing their moon-walking legs inside the set for the first time, they are wanderers in a maze, giddy with the strangeness of encountering furniture where there hadn't been any before, in rooms that seem big where they ought to be small and small where they ought to be big, and wherever they look there are walls, real walls, that seem to have leaped from the floor tapes they're used to, laid out in a pattern on the floor. Those were "walls" you could see through, you knew where you were going before you went there, but this is like blindman's buff: they drift around corners, bump into each other, laugh, shake hands, move on, weightless astronauts softly colliding. The hall seems always full of Joanne carrying a tray somewhere, and Paul taps his way around with his shepherd's crook, wondering, as I do, whenever he opens a door, "Who *are* those guys?"

PAUL: Hey, where's Newman? He's in makeup. They're making up his elbows 'cause he doesn't know where to stand, so his elbows are going to be in every shot.

Michael is describing his shot plan to David Ray, as well as his anxiety about it. John Malkovich, being playful, snatches an exposure meter from a camera assistant and darts from light to light, measuring densities, striking glamour poses: "Which is my best side, Michael, do I look good here?" Paul locates Tony Walton, who presides over the proceedings like the amiable keeper of an inn on its opening day, and gives Tony his wordiest compliment:

PAUL: It's nifty. It all reads.

Tony is quick to mention that John Kasarda, his art director and an associate since *Pippin* days, had plenty to do with it, and so did Susan Bode, who decorated the sets. Both of these people, Tony explains, "are unusually sensitive to the very special nature of this piece."

Michael calls for a fixture to be hoisted above the glass menagerie as "a source of shimmer" for the animals. He has added his son to the camera crew, a tall Byronic-looking young man whose perfect name is Florian, and who will assist him.

PAUL: Michael! You sure you want to go through with this? It's not too late to back out. Do you want to negotiate about our opening for a couple of days, or should we put on the gloves and go at it right now?

MICHAEL: I am ready.

They disappear into the tall gloom of the kitchen. It won't be until I see the film that I'll know that Paul has prevailed. The prop master goes by, looking like one of the wax portrait figurines that El Greco used as models when he painted by candlelight.

Joanne has gone to knit in Amanda's bedroom, where all makeup and hair will also be done, and pats the canvas chair beside her for me to sit down. JOANNE WOODWARD is stenciled on its back. I'm surprised to find that her private retreat will be used for other functions; I'd need some mystical connection to this room if it were mine, if it were to house a character I was playing—but it's only a set to her, she seems to say as she taps the canvas chair again, only a set until her "invisible threshold" rises before her and she finds Amanda on the other side, and home. She would like to take me up on my offer to cook a "family meal" for the *Menagerie* gang and all their husbands and wives. I suggest meatloaf and corn pudding. Her sigh is so ecstatic that she nearly plunges a knitting needle into her heart. She says she stayed up to watch the World Series last night and has fallen hard for Len Dykstra, but she wishes he wouldn't chew tobacco, she's worried about what could happen to his lips.

Mary Bailey comes with news that the commissary people will bring lunch in five minutes but they want to know where to lay it out. "In the urinal," Paul suggests. I have mine standing up, with my salad balanced on a light tower. I stop Michael Ballhaus as he goes by, to ask if he's content with the way things are going.

MICHAEL: Always at the beginning of a film, when you are
    working with a new director, it's a little bit uncertain. And

even though I have worked for a long time with Paul on *The Color of Money,* we were in another relationship then, because after all he was the actor and here it is different. But even so, I love him so much that even when he's troubled, I can say to myself, "It will be fine—"

They're about to run the Gentleman Caller scene. Paul asks to have the couch moved back "so we can get used to cheating it for camera." Jim raises his candelabrum and negotiates the unfamiliar gauze drapes between the dining room and parlor.

PAUL: Jim, as you come through, try to set those curtains on fire.

Jim looks stupefied, then smiles.

The Gentleman Caller scene is more real, more intimate in here than it ever was on the rehearsal stage, and is finally the "less and less" Paul wanted.

PAUL: Good! Jim, the singing was wonderful, the way it just
    dwindled out—

JIM: How was my getting up for you, Michael?

MICHAEL: I loved it!

JIM [*to Paul*]: Now how come you don't take a lesson from
    Michael and only use superlatives with me?

PAUL: Fuck off.

The cast and crew relax. I watch Paul seduce them with his bad jokes and his oversalted popcorn, pulling people aside to tell them funny stories he's forgotten he told them already, or that they are the ones who told him the stories in the first place. But his enjoyment is so contagious that they laugh. I wrote a poem for him once that he liked and I'm still waiting for him to recite it back to me as something he heard in a dream:

> *A fabulous movie star am I*
> *Of truly galactic fame—*
> *I'd happily introduce myself*
> *But I don't remember my name!*

Ribald sometimes, delicate sometimes, modest always, he circulates among his people like a corporal lifted suddenly to staff command, dissolving rank with every conversation. The actors feel safe with him because he's as sensitive to them, and respectful of them, as any good angler who wets his hands before taking the fish off the hook. He calls Karen "Madame" today, and Joanne has become "Joanna." He sits in a puddle of orange light, directing with sunglasses on, right into the glare. Without having had to ask for it, Jim is getting the run-through on the set that he so wanted. When the picture is finished he'll visit me to complete his earlier comments about Paul:

JIM: It's nice to be able to feel some kind of intimacy with a director; it doesn't have to be friendship, just that some kind of trust exists. I finally got to feel that way with Paul, but we came a tremendous distance to get there before the communication barrier was broken. Finally I think he kind of said, "I could like this guy," and he went out of his way to let me know it—invited me down to play ping-pong, shoot pool, go to a race at Miami. And it paid off—it let us stop being strangers—so by the time we got to shoot I began to understand what he meant. He had things to say that released me to work in film the way I do on stage, and to know that no matter how many people in the crew are staring at me, wanting to see a result right now, it's my time to create in, experiment in, *live* in, and I don't have to apologize to anyone for taking it. It really happened finally in one long master shot where I had literally all the words. We did it once, we did it twice, we did it three times, but I was stuck in all the old rhythms. The crew was waiting and I was starting to feel terrible about myself. Then Paul said, "Stop. Just stop. We'll break those rhythms! Right from where you are, come at it from someplace else, any place you've never been in rehearsal. Don't plan, don't think, don't rush—take all the time you need and do whatever occurs to you. You know what the scene is. Have a good flight!" And we did a take, and Karen said, "Gee, that was different from anything you ever did before," and I knew it was too! He took me to the place where actors like to be, where you're living in the moment, where you're making believe, unaware of camera and crew, where you've got permission to stay open to inspiration and a million new things can start to happen. And every time we did it, it was different. Better. Unexpected. I didn't have to *think*. After each take Paul would suggest some specific thing I could really *hear,* really build on, invest all of myself in trying it out because I knew he'd never stick me with anything I didn't want to do. I remember being so excited I picked Karen right up off the floor, just lifted her up and said, "This is fun! This is what it's supposed to be all about!" So out of that morass of missed antecedents and miscommunication, and out of that terrible morning in rehearsal, we wound up with what was, in my experience, the best couple of days I ever had. I think Karen feels that way too. No matter what happens with this picture, I have that time with Paul when all of a sudden the curtain lifted and for a couple of days we made music.

When the run-through of the Gentleman Caller scene ends Paul thumps approval with his shepherd's crook and rises against the orange light.

PAUL: It's solid. It's good. What we have to do now, Michael, is just break it up into usable shooting procedure. All right, that's a wrap!

JIM: Well, this is it for me—for a while. Don't ruin the movie before I get back! I'm going to miss the doughnuts most of all. If I don't see you, Merry Christmas, Happy New Year—

PAUL: I don't even want to *joke* about that! Seriously, I'm pleased with everything. Really good work.

MICHAEL: And I am pleased too.

They all troop off the set and their voices soon fade on the stairs. The leaves in Tony Walton's magical little conservatory tremble with the tread of their exit. I look at the floors and they are wonderful: antiqued flowered "linoleum" upon which the scenics have used eight stencils and lavished thirteen colors to achieve the look of age, and here and there are terrible grayed-out scatter rugs, "Orientals" and bargain-basement "Aubussons" as thin as towels in old railroad hotels. The set rests. All the ingredients gleaned over these weeks from thrift shop and florist, gallery and prop shop, and assembled here only last night in a last frantic scramble of artisans and decorators, will now be permitted to steep over the weekend in the kettle of this unifying atmosphere until Monday, when the camera starts to turn.

Epilogue

Saturday, October 25th 1986 Westport, Connecticut
The Day before Filming

The leaves in the Connecticut woods are glorious this weekend. Paul's cold has thickened, and soon after we drove up tonight, while Joanne and I were talking quietly in the kitchen so we wouldn't disturb him, he came trotting down the stairs from bed to see if he was missing anything. He was wearing only a shirt and his Jockey shorts, and a sumptuous blue wool scarf that he had wound around his neck a couple of times and flung over one shoulder in the style of a Venetian gondolier. Joanne shrieked when she saw him, "My God! Take that off! It's a present I'm saving for—*somebody!*" But he stayed to demonstrate, yet again, that opening shot, shuffling in bare feet over the mismatched pine plank floors, his spindly legs barely holding him up, waving a coconut Popsicle for emphasis and rasping like Andy

Devine. Joanne ordered him back to bed and he turned on his heel and went quietly.

Sunday morning. Paul's voice is gone. He lounges in his terry cloth robe barking wheezily at the editorial page of the Sunday *New York Times,* and spurns my suggestion that we all drive back to New York together this afternoon when Joanne goes in to set up a bridal shower for one of her daughter's friends. He wants to stay here in the quiet as long as he can and drive in late, after the evening traffic eases. I realize I want to stay with him, walk in the woods while he rests, and cook him some chicken soup. "Aw, yeah," he says, as he climbs up to bed again. "Let's take care of the little guy." It comes from his favorite line of the week when one of the staff, trying to lighten Paul's depression about the contretemps with Michael, twitted him by turning to everyone else in the room and saying, "Aw, let's hear it for the little guy," and everyone echoed "Aw-w-w!"

Last night, although she was exhausted, Joanne took me on a drive deep into the country, after Paul had been put to bed, to attend a play she had promised to see. Because she could hardly keep her eyes open, and I have a tendency to close mine the minute anyone turns out a light, we took a solemn oath to keep each other awake no matter how soporific the play might turn out to be. I came to in the middle of the second act to find her in a dead sleep beside me, but with the unfailing good manners to have kept her face turned politely to the stage and an attentive smile on her lips. As I reached for her hand to fulfill my oath, I hesitated, for when the picture starts tomorrow, neither she nor Paul will have had a single day of uninterrupted rest in over a year. I let her sleep. She woke up applauding at the end of the act.

Lying in the barn loft after the play, charmed by a shrouded autumn moon sailing quickly down through the trees, I realized that the events I'd requested to witness and had recorded so urgently till yesterday had sped—within hours—into the past, that something had relaxed like the shudder of a tide, and that when I picked up the pen again, it would be to write in different terms, because along with all the imperative dialogues of those rehearsals, my task as a participant had ended too. With so much of the creative work behind them, Paul, Michael, and the actors had built a platform they could tread upon with trust, and while the long process of production would offer its own discoveries and surprises, its own resolutions of conflicts pending, its own compromises, departures, creative accidents, they were entering upon an entirely different phase, and so was I. I would only be looking in on them from time to time, the way an out-of-town uncle looks in on a sleeping child to see if it's kicked off its covers. I knew that Paul, while retaining a steady rein, would be presiding over an ever-loosening set where all could find in the dark their way to the popcorn, and that it would be drenched with precisely the right amount of melted butter poured onto a spoon agitated to splash it in precisely the right way, and that it would be, as usual, oversalted. I knew that my visits would feel more and more like descents into the boiler room of some ship where the stokers had found their own rhythm, their own language, their own in-family jokes, and where life didn't exist beyond the furnace. And I knew I would always be welcomed—but increasingly with that distant cordiality extended by horses to someone with only a half-remembered scent.

October 27, 1986 Stage H
The First Day of Filming

When I arrived on the set, hours after they'd started—because I was looking for flowers for Joanne—Paul came over with a towel full of Vicks VapoRub wrapped around his throat, to croak two words to me: "John's late." John overslept again, and it isn't until nearly one o'clock that we hear he has arrived at makeup. The rumor is that his alarm clock didn't work, or that it left town again with his lady. When he arrives on the set Paul asks him what went wrong. "I worry a lot at night," John explains. "I didn't fall asleep till five." "Well, I wake up at five and start worrying then," Paul says, "so why don't we both just switch?" When he returns from makeup a few minutes later, John is all smiles, all jokes, and no one ever mentions directly the loss of a whole morning's work.

They make the first official shot of the picture after lunch. Joanne, chatting merrily as Amanda while take after take goes by and plate after plate of a particularly pungent tuna casserole is set before her, treats the filming almost as an interruption in social intercourse and slides back and forth between Amanda's conversation and her own with an astonishingly lubricated ease. Between takes she sits in her 1920s dress of brown velvet on Amanda's threadbare divan, knitting another sweater for a friend and showing no sign of first-day nerves. When they set up for the second shot, some of us adjourn to the flickering monitor in the darkened kitchen. Michael, relieved to be off his feet for a moment, sags onto an apple box, and Florian kneels beside him. David Ray sits back in the shadows against the sink, and Tony Walton—the Herr Drosselmeyer of all these proceedings— stands above everyone, awash in the monitor's blue light. With Joanne on its screen in black-and-white, trilling at Tom to "Chew, chew, chew!" in a voice made mechanical by earphones, it's hard to imagine that she's just over the wall, in the flesh and in living color. Paul calls "Print!" then asks what few directors ever ask their actors: "Do any of you want another take before we break this setup?" I see John nod from his place at the table. Paul calls for quiet, the warning bell is rung, which means the red light of silence has gone on outside the stage, and the scene is repeated. It's a big improvement.

Whenever Paul says "Cut!" and the bell for release is rung, there's always the same shifting of bodies and trampling of feet, as though everyone had different planes to catch at different gates, and because we are on platforms eight feet up, people sound as though they're walking on tom-toms. Burtt Harris, having noticed Paul's flicker of annoyance, but still looking particularly amiable and relaxed, calls his production assistants into a huddle—bright, eager young women mostly—and says, without raising his voice or changing demeanor, "Just as a matter of procedure, I'd appreciate it if you'd find out who the noisemakers are, nail them and their feet to the floor, and ask them to shut the fuck up, so we can have some fucking quiet for this director." They scatter into the trenches and pass the word, and from the next bell on, whenever Paul says "Roll 'em," the soundstage goes into gridlock; men freeze wherever they are, with whatever they have in hand, until he says "Cut!" again.

Karen appears in close-up. The face on the monitor is startling: I can see what they mean when they say that an actor "screens." Her eyes are like tide pools, transparent, reflective, subtle, crammed with life, and the tracks of a hundred different thoughts crisscross their surfaces. Michael, returning to claim his apple box, exclaims, when he sees the monitor, "What eyes! What amazing eyes!" The bell again. Paul's "Action!" is so discreet that I can't even be certain he said it.

Between bells I drift with the rest, needing motion. I go down the steps. I walk around the raw outside walls of the set. The equipment they need surrounds it in neat piles, arranged by species like circus animals at their tie-ups outside the big top, available for call. I come to the alley to which Tom's fire escape descends. The cardboard brick wall of the Paradise Dance Hall is anchored to the floor of the stage by a line of antique radiators, torn out of a tenement somewhere and given second life. The bell, and everyone sits on whatever's available: musical chairs. Sitting all day on a set, as still as stone; with cables snaking around your feet and the midriffs of technicians bellying by; abandoned to blackness as sharp as moonshadows, or drenched in blinding light; stuffing yourself with pastries because there's nothing else quiet to do; taking huge and famished breaths when the blowers come on between takes—all combine to create a state of resigned suspension akin to the limbo of airports when it seems no plane will ever fly again. Curiosity, intelligence, appetite, pulse, plans, hopes are all vaporized in the lights and you sit, reading obituaries as if they were headlines, feeling your beard grow or your lipstick cake depending on who you are, and grateful for those occasional waves of anxiety that let you know you're alive, or will be, if they ever let you out.

Eventually the day ends. At six o'clock Paul has a tub of drinks wheeled in and raises a beer in salutation to the crew, to thank them for a good first day and to launch the picture. Then he calls Malkovich over and, with an air of grave ceremony, presents him with a gift he has somehow found the time and the wit to arrange for: a plastic shopping bag from which he plucks, one by one, a half dozen brand-new alarm clocks of as many makes and sizes, all expensive and beautiful. "For you, John," he says. "I want you to take them home and put them in every room in your house. May they in unison bong, clang, buzz, bang, or grunt and inspire your ass to get in here on time tomorrow morning, for punctuality is the courtesy of kings."

November 7, 1986 Stage H

I have come back from a visit to Seattle after nearly two weeks away. The set feels lived-in now and it has its own smell—stale and homey and sweet, like an old pub. John comes sidling in, making his way through electricians setting lights; he looks sullen and full of a world-weary sensuality, as if he'd just torn loose from an East Village lamppost after beating off under his coat. I don't know where he finds that inner "thing" to exude for Tom—it comes out of Tom's pores, not his own. He reclines on the couch, pursing his lips and asking loudly of no one in particular, "Where's my mama and my hairdresser and everybody?"

"I think," Mary Bailey tells me a little later, "that interpretation came from John. There was a discussion of it early in rehearsal, of Tom's homosexuality, and I remember Paul responded as though John had told him a not-very-nice story about Tennessee Williams. You know, mock shock. 'How can you say that about this character!' John kept playing it and it worked wonderfully. I credit Paul with being able to handle it because I think it was pretty foreign to him at first. And given John's efflorescence, it could have gone in a very wrong direction. Paul protected himself by doing more takes. The impulse came from John, but the control from Paul."

Joanne arrives and sits on the couch by John's feet. "New York has five boroughs, did you know that?" he asks her. "And lots of bridges too, even though all those boroughs are not islands. Can you say them?" "Queens, Manhattan, the Bronx, Brooklyn—and—uh—" "Richmond!" he crows, "but that's very good, Mother! You know so much!" The hairdresser arrives to comb his wig. "Am I fine like this, with my legs like this so you can smell my feet?" he asks Joanne. "Oh, my! This lemon!" she says, ignoring him as she sips her tea. "Do you know that lemon that's been soaking in tea is perfectly delicious?" "You are just awesome, Mother," John says.

Paul and Michael arrive. "Ready whenever you are, fellas," Paul says as he takes a position by the camera. "I'm just along for the ride." They are filming the middle of the Annunciation scene, and John lies with a petulant arm on the back of the sofa like the early portrait of Truman Capote on the dust jacket of *Other Voices, Other Rooms.* With his soft curl of hair, his small catlike smile, his eyelashes batting as he teases her about the coming of the gentleman caller, Tom is a sly, self-satisfied courtesan. Paul calls, "Roil 'em! Roil 'em," and the camera starts to turn. Then he sees that I'm back and comes to greet me. As the film reaches speed, he whispers, "Watch John. You think he's a little fey? Will he fly?" He laughs at the end of the take and says, "That's a print," then tries for another: "Encore, Grand-père, encore!" Each time they do it, John plays it straighter, and every time it's a print, giving Paul options to work with in the cutting room, a broad range of colors he can choose from.

Between setups I join Joanne in Amanda's bedroom, and, like all her places of private retreat, it's jammed with people. All you can hear is the clickety-clack of knitting needles—Joanne's, the hairdresser's, the makeup man's—she has enrolled them all in her Never Be Inactive for a Moment Club. John sits gazing with scientific interest at a woman who is laboring over a Christmas stocking so long that it seems to have no end. It's like a Charles Addams cartoon. When they are ready for Joanne, and her companions put down their knitting and descend on her with brush and sponge and powder, Paul appears in the doorway and winks at me as if to say, "Watch this." Teasingly, he inches a silver Japanese fan from behind his back and tosses it to John as a subtle reminder to keep it down for the rest of the morning's work. Quick to get it, John sinks back amongst the pillows, snaps the fan open, and stares so hard and so coquettishly at Paul that all Paul can do is give a helpless little shrug and hurry off as fast as he can. John laughs. The actors are called to the set. "Come on, Son," Joanne says, putting down her knitting. "Yes, Mother," John replies submissively, and pads after her behind his fan like a homeward-bound geisha at the end of a busy night. Joanne looks back at him and laughs. "My God!" she cries. "It's Clifton Webb and May!"

During a break I see that Paul has crawled into Tom's bedroom like a wounded fox to its den and lies resting in the dark on Tom's cot. Only his shoes are visible sticking out of the tangle of bedclothes, and I can make out the weary rise and fall of his breathing. Before a minute has gone, they are calling him again.

November 18, 1986

The banquet for the cast and a number of guests was given tonight at the Newmans' Fifth Avenue apartment. I had prepared it downtown at the small *pied-à-terre* where I am staying, and worked the borrowed Cuisinart till the wires nearly smoked. At three o'clock this morning I realized with a start that there were no pans large enough to bake anything in, or to transport it to where it *could* be baked, so today I dumped all of it, uncooked, into plastic garbage bags, all thirty pounds of meatloaf, corn pudding, rutabaga puree, and what I hoped would be the airiest of tapiocas, dumped the bags into my one large suitcase, then threw the whole slithering mess onto a Madison Avenue bus. I rode with my feet on the suitcase all the way uptown while its contents tossed and writhed beneath my soles like something not quite murdered that was reviving to haunt me.

The only noteworthy thing about the evening, which had that halting atmosphere that sometimes comes when actors have no dialogue to say and unfamiliar spouses join the clan, was a remarkable encounter between John Malkovich and the tapioca. By some mysterious twist of childhood, tapioca had never entered his life, and now, as bowl after bowl of it wobbled by on its way up the table, he seemed to grow more and more apprehensive. When the passing stopped, and he found himself staring into his own bowl, his agitation became actual alarm. Abruptly shoving his chair back to provide a ready avenue of escape, he studied the thing that confronted him as if to seek out its intentions, touched it experimentally with a finger which, upon contact, he instantly withdrew, shuddered once, rose up with a stricken cry, "I think I'm going to let it win!" and fled, ashen-faced, into another room.

December 4, 1986

Paul and I spent a hurried day in Connecticut, with Paul driving both ways at such hair-raising speed that I had to say my Now-I-lay-mes. Hurtling back to the city, I asked how some of the issues on *The Glass Menagerie* had been resolved, for the shooting is history now and the roughly assembled film and its outtakes stand in rows of cans on the shelves of the editing room where Paul and David Ray will disappear to make the movie. "Looking back on it now, and remembering Michael's excitement about the wonderful things he wanted to do with memory, do you think he was able to accomplish that? Was he given the freedom?" "I come back to the present for the monologues," Paul says, "but the light's not really definable: it could be day or night, so time is vague. Objects are vague." I try again: "And his circular dolly shot at the beginning—did you do that?" "Didn't work," Paul says. "Once I got on the set I realized that it wouldn't hold to carry any long dolly shot all the way around that apartment. So I wipe—in opposite directions as Tom explores the place. Sometimes he's coming right to left, a second later from left to right. And I do the same with what he sees: moving shots of things in the past and present, seen from his point of view. The effect is opposition, disorientation. I don't know how it's going to work. Tomorrow we're going to see the first rough cut, without opticals, music, or effects. It's going to be very jerky. David Ray's smart. He's not trying to impress you or anybody else who's going to be there. He's just stuck everything in, pieces of all the film I shot, to show me what I have and remind me what angles I'll have to work with when we really start editing. I don't know how it's going to look." "You mean you haven't seen it before?" I ask him. "Uh-uh," he says. "Tomorrow will be the first time."

Once back at the apartment he left me in the den while he went to get a handful of pretzels, and never came back. After half an hour or so, I called out to ask where he'd gone. "I are here," came the reply from not very far away. He was out on the terrace, with the door wide open and the curtains blowing, staring down at the park. There was nothing he could do until tomorrow.

December 5, 1986

I'm to see *The Glass Menagerie* this morning and to meet Paul here in the lobby of the lab at ten o'clock. He rushes in three minutes late, muttering incantations against the traffic and charged with a kind of heady energy. He's carrying his big tote bag full of things he can't possibly need today, and probably picked it up by mistake on his way to the cab. "This picture's going to wind up in libraries!" he growls as the elevator creaks its way up. "Probably no one will ever want to see it." "Where to again?" asks the elevator operator without any recognition of Paul. "*Glass Menagerie*," Paul repeats. It is obviously not a title on everybody's lips. We are let out on the ninth floor and hump down the hall to a theatre packed with strangers who turn faces to us as blank as those golden masks of expectation in *The Royal Hunt of the Sun*. Wrong movie, wrong theatre, wrong floor. We try another one. "I did it for Joanne," Paul says as the elevator ticks down. "That performance deserved to be on film." We stop somewhere. "The moment of truth," says Paul as he leads me out. I volunteer that the marvelous thing about moviemaking is that there are so *many* moments of truth, a new one with every new cut of a film: a motion picture is a process, a series of continuous corrections—very much like life—never completed, merely stopped at a certain point, and if fulfilling, stopped too soon.

We pass through a well-appointed waiting room, Paul striding ahead, and gather up David Ray, Burtt Harris, Tony Walton, Marcia Franklin, and Joe Caracciolo, who have been standing with lowered heads, like cattle expecting rain. We all take separate seats in separate rows. Joanne has refused to come. "I know what it *felt* like," she says of her acting, "so I don't need to see what it *looks* like." My heart is pounding away; it always does at these things. What will I say if I don't like it, after all their effort? There's a terrible edgy goodwill at bad screenings in Hollywood, and a sound of morbid expectancy like the high, light whine of an incoming shell that fails to explode, and people say, "Great!" between their teeth, and shake hands with the tips of their fingers, and flee to their cars to consult before they have to give opinions. But here we are, just six of us and highly visible to Paul: four colleagues, his office assistant, and me. No place to hide.

As the lights go down I say a final Now-I-lay-me and bless everybody involved. The picture starts, all vaguely familiar, and it has a lovely look. I think John has been muted too much—the wildness, the irreverence and comedy of his most eccentric choices seem smoothed out by the use of only the most "acceptable" takes, or perhaps he never repeated what I saw in rehearsal. Joanne is incandescent, sidestepping stardom in every way she can. She has always acted for the ensemble and has made this the story of a family struggling in a burrow too deep for light. Perhaps it's generosity that makes the difference between actress and prima donna, and this is a most generous performance. I wait for catharsis. Did Laurette Taylor make me cry? I remember only a shuffling little char with a consumptive's cough, hair in a dustrag, ravaged moonface luminous with hope. She never seemed to be acting, but rather to have simply wandered in from some employment agency up the street, found a chair that looked comfortable and happened to be on the stage, and sat down in it to offer me all of her soul. But did she make me cry? Joanne does, on "Jonquils," and Karen and Jim do with that kiss that begins Laura's life and with the one that never comes, and ends it. Increasingly I'm aware of Paul's restraint. He has left the light on Tennessee, not stood in it himself. He will not manipulate emotion. In my mind I hear him saying, as he has so often said, "Never repeat an emotion. Time it. Do it once. Then let it alone." When will it come, that "once"? Who will be its messenger this time? Then suddenly it's there. It's Malkovich. Fighting hard to sit on the heartbreak, way down the line in the very last frames of the film, a dusty, bearded figure in a derelict place, a brother exhumed and freezing, caught in a shaft of chilly light and offering us one tear. One. "Blow out your candles, Laura." The tear falls. His. Then mine, for I am undone.

All of my own regrets are stirred by his, all of the moments when I might have been more loving, or taken a moment to understand, or to make amends. My own lost sister is with me. Is it for her or for Laura that I weep? Or for myself? Blow out your candles, all of you, and rest. John has done this for us. And Paul. By holding until that moment Paul lets us see, long after they have passed us, the emotion stored in every preceding scene: all are remembered now, bathed in the ache of that ending. He has taken a great risk in waiting, and in having the faith that John, if given the room to come to his own experience of pain, would provide in a moment that took only five minutes to film, the meaning of the picture and the yearning for forgiveness in our hearts. "As far as the ending is concerned," Paul had said at the beginning, "the best thing I've got is Malkovich and his emotion."

No one can speak. The lights come up gingerly, but still nobody moves or looks at Paul. We sit rigidly, staring straight ahead at the empty screen. Minutes go by. Tony Walton is the first to find his feet, but not his voice. He makes his way to the back row where Paul has been sitting all alone and whispers something to him I can't hear. Paul falls in half like a hinge, forward, nearly out of his seat. It is his first news from the outside world that the picture works. The rest of us stand up and try to say things. Because he is modest I'm always astonished by the depth of the art in him. I mumble something: "This is the only production I've seen since the play was written that really honors Tennessee, by not being afraid to portray him as he might have been growing up," but it's all dead words and I can't finish. It's like trying to sing "Glory, Glory Hallelujah" with all those people holding your hands as you walked through the streets of Montgomery at the end of the Selma march—you just couldn't get through it, you'd strangle on the tune. The others crowd in with their congratulations, all these hardworking colleagues who have gone such a distance with him, and I withdraw. As I watch them all together I think of Mary Bailey and what she told me the other night:

"There were people who said, 'He doesn't know what he wants and he doesn't know when he's got it,' in reference to the number of takes he'd make, but nothing slipped by. He kept tabs on all the elements all the time. I would say forthrightness is his great strength; he is absolutely fearless in giving the whole story to whoever it is he's dealing with. And I think he's a poet, too—an embarrassed poet with a feeling for the universe. He spends a lot of time undermining himself; I suppose he has to. But I have the sense that he's still in the process of discovering who he is, and I think that's remarkable because most people in Paul's position have swallowed their own mythology. But he's still open, still free, in the radical sense of being free in the world. He's not embarrassed to be one of the guys and tell awful jokes, but he's terribly shy somehow about the way he responds to beautiful things: he's reticent to show just how sensitive he is. There was a time we weren't sure we wanted the phonograph in a shot, and Michael said, 'It's just an old Victrola.' Paul said, 'I love those old things, I love those old things!' A record was playing on it, and the record was 'It Seems Like Old Times.' "

The crowd around him dissolves and there is room for me again. I look at him, this sweet uncertain man, this least showy of artists, this elegant friend, and I can only bite down hard on the wave of appreciation that chokes me, and rather formally shake his hand.

Appendix
SYNOPSIS OF
THE GLASS MENAGERIE

Scene One: The Dinner Scene

Tom Wingfield, a poet and the narrator of the play who promises "truth in the pleasant disguise of illusion," introduces us to an alley in St. Louis, where he lived during the Depression in an apartment he ran away from at twenty-one. He is there to conjure the memory of a painful time when "the world was waiting for bombardments" and he was waiting to escape— from his overwhelming mother, Amanda, and his crippled sister, Laura, who broke his heart.

He takes us back to a certain noonday meal: Amanda is urging him not to bolt his food, but to "Chew, chew!" so he can savor every mouthful leisurely. His appetite is ruined by her "hawklike attention" to every bite he takes, and he rushes from the table for a smoke. Amanda fusses over Laura as she waits on her: she must keep herself fresh in case a gentleman caller comes.

When he hears his mother recount, for the hundredth time, how on a special summer Sunday afternoon in Blue Mountain when she was a girl, seventeen gentlemen callers came calling, Tom groans. But Laura, needing serenity, beseeches him to indulge Amanda in reciting memories that lighten her despair. The sight of her husband's portrait on the wall, a charmer who worked for the telephone company before he "fell in love with long distance" and ran away, brings Amanda rudely back to the present. She trills at Laura to practice her typing till a gentleman caller comes, but Laura, believing that none will ever come for her, smiles at her brother with a rueful truth: "Mother's afraid I'm going to be an old maid."

Scene Two: The Deception Scene

Laura is playing with her "glass menagerie," a collection of "the tiniest little animals in the world," when she is startled by her mother's early return. When Laura pretends to be practicing her typing, Amanda, crying, "Deception, Deception," as she pulls off her coat, tells her she has found out the truth: stopping at Rubicam's Business College just now to ask how her daughter was faring, she was informed by the typing teacher that Laura has been absent all semester—the *pressure* had made her sick! What was she doing all that time she was pretending to be at school? Amanda demands. She walked, Laura confesses. Walked, found warmth at the conservatory in the park, shelter in the bird house at the zoo. In such avoidance Amanda foresees for them both a future of abject dependency, for with the loss of that fifty-dollar tuition, and what it signifies about Laura's dependability, go all the hopes and dreams she has ever had for the fragile girl—*unless* "that long-delayed but always expected something that we live for" appears, in the form of a gentleman caller who will fall in love with Laura and save them all. Was there never some boy Laura cared for? There was Jim O'Connor, Laura recalls, who sang in *The Pirates of Penzance* at high school and called her Blue Roses when she had "pleurosis" once and he thought she'd called it "blue roses," but that was long ago; he must be married by now.

Caught up in her fantasies of marriage, Amanda silences Laura's description of herself as a "cripple." Why, she has only "a little defect . . . a slight disadvantage" that she can learn to cover with charm. She must "cultivate . . . charm—and vivacity—and *charm!*" It was the one thing her runaway father had plenty of.

Scene Three: The Quarrel Scene

Tom, as narrator, steps out of the drama to tell us how Amanda's obsession with the idea of a gentleman caller's imminent arrival filled her days and drove her to seek that little extra money that would "feather the nest and plume the bird" by soliciting subscriptions over the telephone for the *Homemaker's Companion* magazine.

Phoning everyone on her list of prospective subscribers, Amanda warns Ida Scott that if she doesn't renew her subscription right away it will expire in the middle of a juicy episode of a serial about "the horsey set on Long Island," but Ida remembers she has something in the oven and hangs up.

Now Amanda fusses over Tom as he labors to write a poem: he should have more light, she insists; his posture's wrong; his internal organs are pressing against his "poor little heart!" At last he is driven to explode at her: with all her hovering, her eternal correcting and prodding, he has no place, no thing he can call his own! He is going to the movies! But Amanda is at the end of her patience too, she cries: night after night Tom "goes to the movies" but she knows perfectly well that he's doing out there things he's ashamed to be doing. Coming home drunk! With not enough sleep to sustain him at the warehouse of Continental Shoemakers! Jeopardizing the future for them all! Who pays the rent, he wants to know! How can she keep harping on his selfishness when he's spending his youth on her, and on Laura, working always at something he hates? He would rather have his brains bashed out than work another minute at that warehouse! Nothing will silence her till a wild inspiration hits him: he fixes her with a madman's stare—he doesn't go to the movies, he says, he goes to opium dens! He runs a string of cathouses! People call him El Diablo and his enemies are plotting to dynamite this place! "And will I be glad," he shouts, "Will I be happy! And so will you be. You'll go up—up—over Blue Mountain on a broomstick! With seventeen gentlemen callers. You ugly babbling old witch!" Wounded, Amanda vows never to speak to him again unless he apologizes. Tom hurls his coat across the parlor where it strikes the glass menagerie, then he falls to his knees in contrition. Laura covers her face.

Scene Four: The Drunk Scene

Tom reels home drunk in the middle of the night, rattling a party noisemaker, and drops his key in the dark. The noise of his search brings Laura. He has been to the movies, he tells her: a Garbo movie, and a Mickey Mouse, and a newsreel, and a coming attraction, and a stage show with Malvolio the Magician, who invited Tom to be his assistant and help him turn water into whiskey with the help of a magic scarf. And then Malvolio escaped from a locked coffin without removing a single nail!

Laura, filled with the same tremulous love and concern for Tom that he is feeling for her, leads him to bed and he gives her the magic scarf. From the depth of his own entrapment he sees their existence as being precisely like that of the man in the coffin, but how can anyone ever escape from one without removing a nail?

Scene Five: The Apology Scene

Amanda, clinging fast to her vow of silence, watches Tom blow on the breakfast coffee she has made him as the minutes tick by and they both yearn for truce. At last he blurts out his apology, permitting her to vent her own broken heart in an outburst of regret and praise for her children. She knows she's difficult, she admits, but hers is such a lonely battle, and whatever she might say to Tom, he must know that she looks to him as her "right-hand bower" and he mustn't fail her now: Laura must be saved. There is so much in her heart she can't describe, she tells him. "There's so much in my heart, too," he says, but while it seems for a moment that he might confess his secret, it all dissolves in her nattering: about his drinking, his going to the movies, his failure to lift his mind from gross instincts and dwell on "superior things," and the moment is lost.

He would flee but she snares him with the revelation of a letter found in his drawer, sent him by the Merchant Marine and accepting his application for enlistment. She will not permit him to escape as his father did, she warns, without first providing for Laura. Provide, or produce a gentleman caller! Is there not one young man at the warehouse he can persuade to come home for Sister? Will he do it? Will he? Will he? Will he? "Yes!" comes his strangled cry as he flees her down the stairs.

Amanda hastens to the phone. Would Ella Cartwright con-

sider a subscription to the *Homemaker's Companion?* But Ella
Cartwright, groggy with sleep, can only remind Amanda that it
is seven o'clock in the morning.

Scene Six: The Annunciation Scene

As the narrator, Tom comes onto the fire escape to invoke the
remembered music of the Paradise Dance Hall across the alley,
with its promise of adventure to a generation that adventure
seemed to have passed by, and to recall for us a time when sex
"hung in the gloom like a chandelier and flooded the world with
brief, deceptive rainbows" as it girded itself for war.

In memory again, Amanda joins him on the fire escape under
the "little silver slipper of a moon" they both have wished on,
just rising over Garfinkel's Delicatessen. It is one of those rare
times when they can be easy with each other, almost compan-
ionable, and Tom, delighted by a secret he can barely contain, is
in a teasing mood. He won't tell her what he wished for on the
moon, but he thinks he knows what *she* wished for: a gentleman
caller. Well, one is coming soon. "How soon?" "Quite soon."
"How soon?" "Very, very soon!" Tomorrow, in fact. For supper.
Amanda can scarcely believe it. But tomorrow? With no time
for preparations? With nothing for her, or Laura, to wear? And
who *is* this gentleman caller? A friend from the warehouse, Tom
says, who doesn't drink, isn't married, goes to night school, and
is known as Mr. O'Connor. That means Irish, she cries, and Irish
means fish; she'll make a salmon loaf. She'll put cretonne covers
over everything, and have the lamp she'd been making pay-
ments on sent out.

Even as he teases her, it touches Tom to see her pleased, but he
warns her against expectations. Mr. O'Connor is only expecting
supper; he knows nothing of Laura or of her condition—that she

is crippled and "different from other girls," that she lives in a world of old phonograph records and tiny little animals of glass. It brings up a hurt that neither can cope with, but Amanda, with her wounded heart still resolute, summons Laura to leave the dishes in the sink and come out to wish on the moon, for "Happiness! And just a little bit of good fortune!"

Scene Seven: The Gentleman Caller Scene

As narrator, Tom tells the audience that he has only invited Mr. O'Connor because he's the sole acquaintance Tom has at the warehouse. He remembers him from high school as having been as astonishing as Laura was unobtrusive, a star whose "speed had definitely slowed." He doesn't know if Jim even remembers Laura, or would place her as Tom's sister if he did.

The apartment glows with welcome, its shabbiness disguised under the illusion of his mother's skill. She is helping Laura now to dress by a paper lantern's light, but Laura, looking luminous, thinks Amanda is setting a man-trap when she makes her wear "gay deceivers."

Amanda runs away to dress herself and reappears as a "surprise," displaying the yellowing gown she wore to the cotillion and a fresh bouquet of jonquils in her arms. Flooded with expectations and the fervent memories of her own romantic past, she recalls the giddiness of the summer when malaria fever swept Blue Mountain and she loaded the house with jonquils until every vase was full. "Malaria fever," she sighs, remembering, "your father—and jonquils." But when she mentions the gentleman caller's name, Laura ignites with fear: if it is the same Jim O'Connor she knew in high school she will have to be excused from coming to supper, she couldn't face that Mr. O'Connor while so many feelings persist. But when the doorbell rings, Amanda is in no mood for rebellion and insists that Laura let him in. Besides, she wants to delay her own dramatic entrance.

Jim doesn't remember Laura. Smoking with Tom on the fire escape he tells about the public speaking course he's taking to help him "square up" to people and develop the poise that could be his passport out of the warehouse. Tom says he's got a passport too—his acceptance by the Merchant Marine. He confides that he paid his dues instead of the light bill, but hopes to escape before the current is turned off. "I'm like my father," he explains. "The bastard son of a bastard."

Amanda makes her entrance finally, shocking Tom with her appearance, full of "girlish southern vivacity," prattling about Laura's domesticity in a torrent of little white lies, pretending that Laura has prepared the meal that Amanda cooked and laid on the table herself. Laura, dragged from her hiding place in the kitchen, collapses on arriving at her chair and must be carried to the parlor to recover. Amanda, struggling to save an occasion whose promise is dissolving as swiftly as her dreams, asks Tom to offer grace.

The lights blink off in the middle of supper and its meaning is clear to Amanda. She keeps Tom in the kitchen to help with the dishes and sends Mr. O'Connor to Laura with dandelion wine and candles to light his way.

Laura, trembling with the "almost impossible strain of being alone with a stranger," is coaxed into the candlelight where Jim can try to make friends. It is only when she asks if he still sings that the name Blue Roses comes back to him; she reminds him that she was the crippled girl who made such a clumping sound with her brace when she came to their singing class late, but he denies he ever heard it. He tries to help with her shyness, judges her problem to be "an inferiority complex," and admits that until he took up public speaking, he felt inferior too. She must learn to think of herself as special in some way, he says. Laura believes that her glass collection is special, and she places a fragile glass unicorn carefully in his hand.

A waltz floats in from across the alley, and the gentleman caller asks Laura to dance. It carries her out of her shyness but their brief connection is shattered when Jim, dancing by the table where he has set the little unicorn, brushes against it and sends it shattering onto the floor. Laura assures him that it doesn't matter: without a horn to make it different, it can feel like all the other horses on the shelf. Touched by her sweetness, he tells her she's pretty: Other people are "common as weeds— but you—you're *Blue Roses!* Somebody ought to kiss you, Laura." His kiss transfigures her, but it shames Mr. O'Connor. It was wrong to do it, he says. There are strings on him. He's in love with a girl named Betty. Laura's reply is to give him the injured unicorn and withdraw to her phonograph for sanctuary.

Amanda, not sensing the mood in the room, bursts in with a tray of lemonade. Jim explains the situation hurriedly and leaves. Amanda summons Tom. She berates him for what she thinks was his betrayal, but he turns back the blame and, too weary any longer to explain, leaves for "the movies." "Go!" Amanda shouts after him. "Don't let anything interfere with your selfish pleasure! Just go! Go to the movies! . . . Go to the moon, you selfish dreamer!"

Tom returns to address us for the last time. He didn't go to the moon—he went much farther. But wherever he went the memory of his sister followed. Neither drink, nor the movies, nor brief interludes with strangers could ever blow out her candles, could ever extinguish her light. "Blow out your candles, Laura," he commands, for while they burn no peace can come to him. She blows them out.